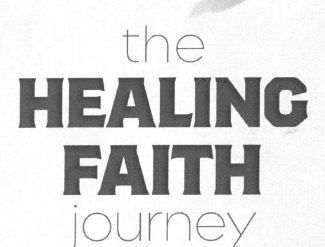

the
HEALING
FAITH
journey

Unless otherwise noted, all scripture references are from the King James Version of the Bible. Public Domain.

The author uses <u>underlined</u> and **bold** type to emphasize words and phrases in certain scripture quotations.

The Healing Faith Journey

Copyright © 2022 by Dale Campbell

ISBN: 979-8-9866855-0-2

Library of Congress Control Number: 2022915579

First Paperback Edition: 2022

Dale Campbell Publications

911 TLC Lane, London, KY 40741

www.graceforyou.com

"My son, attend to my words; incline thine ear unto my sayings. Let them not depart from thine eyes; keep them in the midst of thine heart. For they are life unto those that find them, and health to all their flesh. Keep thy heart with all diligence; for out of it are the issues of life."

PROVERBS 4:20-23

CONTENTS

DEDICATION

This book is dedicated to...

My loving wife, Patty, who has stood by my side in faith and ministry throughout the years. She has been my caregiver, coach, and prayer partner during my physical battles, and her unwavering stand in agreement with me was essential to our victory in this good fight of faith.

My children, Mikaela and Zachary, and my son-in-law, Grant, who now serve alongside me in ministry. They are always a strength and encouragement as we embrace our future by faith.

My Grace Fellowship family, who have stood beside me in prayer and support. I will always be mindful of your prayers of agreement, encouraging words, and every token of support during my healing journey of faith.

Bridgette Smith who has dedicated herself to numerous hours of editing, formatting, and other necessary tasks to preserve my testimony and make the message of faith and healing available to those who read this book.

FOREWORD

by Audrey Mack

I am blessed and honored to recommend this book on divine healing. I first met Pastor Dale Campbell when he invited me to minister at his church, Grace Fellowship, on the subject of divine healing. At the time, he was still on his healing journey, and I encountered a man who was full of peace, full of faith, and who walked sensitive to the Holy Spirit while remaining honest and authentic. In this book, he is not afraid to share the questions – and the struggles – he had while fighting the good fight of faith. This book is filled with the word of God and will build up your faith while showing you how to allow the Holy Spirit to lead you through your own healing journey.

Whether you are seeking healing, are healthy, or want to help someone else, this book is a great tool and very easy reading. I started reading and could not put it down, as my spirit was bearing witness with everything I read. Thank you, Pastor Dale, for sharing such profound truths with such simplicity. Your book is a gift to the Body of Christ!

Audrey C. Mack
Founder & President, GoTell Ministries, Inc.

INTRODUCTION

The great miracles found throughout the Bible have intrigued me since a very early age. As a small boy growing up in a rural Baptist church, I remember looking through the pages of the New Testament and discovering tremendous promises, such as Matthew 17:20, which declares: *"if ye have faith as a grain of mustard seed, ye shall say unto this mountain, Remove hence to yonder place; and it shall remove; and nothing shall be impossible unto you…"* and Luke 18:27 that says: *"…the things which are impossible with men are possible with God.*" I also found the Gospels filled with examples of the many miracles of Jesus. Yet, the church I grew up in never emphasized these passages, and I often wondered why.

Although the Lord's mighty works of healing and deliverance were explored in our Sunday school classes and, occasionally, through the pastor's sermons, we never seemed to truly grasp how the same Jesus who performed such great miracles during Bible times could – and would – do the same for us today. Interestingly, I do not recall ever seeing any healings or miracles take place in that church. However, this lack of the miraculous does not come as a surprise, as the Lord has since taught me something very important:

THOSE THINGS NEVER PREACHED WILL NEVER BE EXPERIENCED.

In December of 1984, my wife, Patty, and I began our ministry. From the start, I always included the preaching of faith, healing, and miracles as we traveled and held revivals in various churches. I believed that if Jesus was interested in the sick while on earth, He must still be interested in the sick of the present age. Just as the writer of Hebrews declares: *"Jesus Christ the same yesterday, and today, and forever"* (Hebrews 13:8), I also trusted that if God was a God of miracles in the Bible, He MUST still be a God of miracles today. I was convinced healing belonged to believers and faith was the key to receiving, even though I had learned very little about faith and healing growing up.

The only reference point I had for my beliefs was the word of God. I did not know any faith-healing evangelists. I did not come from a family of ministers. My roots were in a traditional Baptist church where my father and grandfather both served as deacons. Yet, despite my background, God called me out to be a first-generation Pentecostal preacher of His word – a word that included the Baptism of the Holy Spirit and the word of faith regarding healing and miracles.

Although I had never needed healing or a miracle when my ministry began, that would eventually change. Over the years, I have experienced symptoms of multiple sclerosis (MS), major depression with a chemical imbalance, and even leukemia. Yet, faith in God's word and divine healing has brought me through each time. In this book, I will discuss how God's supernatural touch helped me to overcome these serious physical and emotional trials. More importantly, I will also share some of the many truths regarding healing I have learned from God's word along this journey. I remain convinced – now more than ever – that God's healing power is still available to His Church today. I encourage you to build your faith in God's word for your healing.

You, too, can be healed!

CHAPTER 1

God's Word: The Necessary Foundation

Everything we receive from the Lord comes through the avenue of faith. Most Christians understand this truth, albeit their insight may be limited to certain facets. For example, in my small country church, we did not have much insight into the things of the Holy Spirit or the possibilities of healings and miracles. However, we did have a great understanding of how our salvation comes by faith through God's grace. As the Apostle Paul wrote in Ephesians: *"For by grace are ye saved through faith...* " (Eph. 2:8). Yet, while we had faith for salvation, we had little faith for anything else. Oh, how great it would have been if we had also understood how the faith that saves us is also capable of manifesting healing for us! The book of Hebrews gives excellent insight into the power of faith in the Christian's life:

> *"Now faith is the substance of things hoped for, the evidence of things not seen."*
>
> HEBREWS 11:1

Faith stands in the place of what we are believing for until that belief becomes a reality in the natural world. For example, let us say I am believing in faith for an issue with my back to be healed. Faith believes I am healed until it becomes a reality in the flesh and no more pain is present. To have faith does not mean I instantly experience the full manifestation of that for which I am believing. On the contrary, the process is sometimes quite the opposite. Faith may have to stand for an indefinite season of time, with the only evidence of having received what you are believing for being a promise from the word of God. The good news is that having a word or promise from God is enough!

WHAT IS BIBLE FAITH?

One of the greatest causes of failure in receiving that for which we are believing is a misguided interpretation of what faith is and what it is not. Bible faith is uniquely different from how the world sees faith – and even how many in the Church view faith. Simply put, biblical faith requires the use of the Bible. Our faith must be genuine, biblical faith, as defined in scripture, to produce supernatural results. The Apostle Paul gives us a great revelation as to what real Bible faith is:

"So then _faith_ cometh by _hearing,_ and hearing by the _word of God."_

ROMANS 10:17

Simply put, NO WORD = NO FAITH. Bible faith comes ONLY by hearing the word of God, and the word is the foundation upon which biblical faith is built and from which such faith continues to grow. Sadly, many people try to have faith – and even think they are in faith – only to discover their faith has NO FOUNDATION on which to stand. Bible faith is not saying *"I hope so"* or merely *"wishing"* something will happen. It is not ignoring the circumstances and hoping things will change or symptoms will disappear. Biblical faith does not ask as many people as possible to pray in hopes that someone can *"get a prayer through"* to God. No, Bible faith has much more certainty. Biblical faith has confidence! Why? Because it is established and built upon the SURE foundation of the word of God – and no safer footing to stand upon exists. You can be certain of what God has promised you. Because God's indisputable word is the foundation of Bible faith, we can have the confidence to receive, even if our circumstances remain the same.

When speaking with those facing issues and circumstances related to their health, I often hear them say they are *"in faith."* Yet this statement often only comes after the individual has talked at length about their symptoms or repeated every negative thing the doctor has told them about their situation.

For example, someone might tell me: *"Pastor, I have an incurable tumor. The doctors say I only have six months to live, but I believe God will heal me."* These people can talk at length about the pain or symptoms in their bodies, repeating every detail of what doctors have said about their health. Often, such individuals can even give a very in-depth description of their disease or diagnosis – many times due to their having done hours of *"research"* about it on the Internet. Yet, many of these same individuals who say they are *"in faith"* after rattling off the details of their ailments cannot quote even five healing scriptures from the word of God. They might be good people or faithful church attendees, but such individuals are not in BIBLICAL faith! The foundation of Bible faith MUST be the word of God.

Again, as I stated earlier: NO WORD = NO FAITH. Many are deceived into thinking they are in faith simply because they believe in God, while others are misled by a false, non-biblical faith that only believes God *"can"* do something. Bible faith not only believes in God and that He is able, but it also believes God has ALREADY DONE what He has promised! Bible faith believes things ARE done, not things WILL BE done!

Take Abraham, for example. When God promised him a son, Abraham neither considered the aging condition of his one-hundred-year-old body nor the condition of his similarly aged wife, Sarah. Instead, his only consideration was what God had said:

> *"And being fully persuaded that, what he had promised, he was able also to perform."*
>
> ROMANS 4:21

And what was God's promise to Abraham? Simply:

*"...as it is written, I have made
thee a father of many nations..."*

ROMANS 4:17

This word from God, as well as others, became the
foundation of Abraham's faith. Without God's promise,
Abraham would not have had any reason to believe
he would ever become a father of anyone, much less a
father of nations.

SPEND TIME BUILDING YOUR FOUNDATION

We must spend time building our faith foundation. The
only means of genuine faith is the word of God. To build
our foundation of faith, we must give ourselves over to
spending much time in His word. Most Christians spend
little to no time reading or studying the Bible. Despite
living in an era when the Internet, smartphones, and
other devices give us unlimited ways to read, watch, or
listen to God's word, the response of many is still: *"I just*

don't have time." Sadly, when trouble arises – such as a sickness or disease requiring a miracle – many discover very quickly their faith foundation is either nonexistent or so weak it cannot produce the results necessary to overcome their circumstances. In some instances, cancer can grow faster than faith, which is why we should not wait until the need is present to begin growing our faith. Do not wait until you receive a death sentence from the doctor. If you do, you may not have time to build your foundation of faith quickly enough. Building a foundation takes time!

Some time ago, I was in a city where a new high-rise building was under construction downtown. At first, the project seemed to be going nowhere. Despite the presence of an enormous hole in the ground surrounded by all sorts of activity, I could see nothing demonstrating actual progress when I passed by. However, many months later, I returned to the construction site and saw, much to my surprise, a massive framework of steel reaching several stories into the air. What I initially failed to consider in the beginning was the amount of time necessary for constructing the structure's foundation. Indeed, once the workers laid the foundation, the progress being made on the building quickly became much more apparent. In the same sense, seasons without visible signs of progress will always be present when building our foundation of faith. Just as the groundwork for a high rise takes time to complete, creating a strong foundation of faith will not happen overnight! You must begin now and see it through daily. The good news is, when you spend time building your foundation and trouble arises, you will have a place to stand!

BECOME AGGRESSIVE IN FAITH

In August 2015, I received a diagnosis of chronic lymphocytic leukemia (CLL). Under normal conditions, this disease would have progressed slowly and possibly never needed treatment. However, by January of 2017, the CLL was out of control in my body and causing severe issues, with one oncologist determining I was already at Stage IV of the disease. While a normal hemoglobin level is 12.5 to 13 or above, mine was at 4.5 or less, so low that I required emergency blood transfusions just to stay alive. After conducting several tests, including a bone marrow biopsy, my oncologist concluded the disease had taken on an unusual and extremely aggressive form, possibly due to my genetics. As a result, I began immediate treatment, including chemotherapy.

I will share more details about my experience with CLL later. However, I mention it now to illustrate the importance of building a strong foundation of faith BEFORE trouble arises. I am sure my outcome would not have been as positive had Patty and I not taken the time to build our foundation for healing. Although I already had a good, basic faith foundation based on God's promises, Patty and I became much more aggressive with our faith when I received the initial CLL diagnosis in 2015. We realized:

WORDS ARE SEEDS, AND EVERY SEED HAS A HARVEST.

Words of faith act as *"seeds"* to produce a harvest of faith, while words of doubt and fear yield a harvest of fear and unbelief. The words we allow to be sown into our lives through what we hear, see, or say will eventually bear fruit. Thus, we knew we could not be in faith – and stay in faith – while listening to unbelief. We purposely spent considerably less time watching secular television. YouTube and streaming devices, such as Roku, became great tools for building our faith, BUT we were very selective of to whom and to what we listened or watched. Even my office routine changed. Every morning I would arrive at the church by 8:30 AM, and I would spend most of the morning – and sometimes most of the afternoon – in the word of God. I did this by reading the word, listening to the word, watching faith-filled sermons, and speaking the word aloud. I was building my faith foundation! During this time, I began to take Proverbs 4 very seriously:

> "My son, attend to <u>my words</u>; incline thine ear unto my sayings. Let them not depart from thine eyes; keep them in the midst of thine heart. For they <u>are life</u> unto those that find them, <u>and health to all their flesh</u>. Keep thy heart with all diligence, for out of it are the issues of life."
>
> PROVERBS 4:20-23

I was wholly convinced the Holy Scriptures were life and health to my flesh. I received the precious promises of God as my medicine, and it worked! God later spoke to my heart and drew my attention to three things every believer should do daily:

1. **LOOK** AT THE WORD OF GOD

    We should keep the word of God going into our eyes by LOOKING at the promises of God for ourselves. Sometimes we are guilty of quoting verses from memory but never actually setting our eyes on the actual scriptures. Take time to look up the promises and fix your eyes on the living word of God!

2. **LISTEN** TO THE WORD OF GOD
We need to hear the word of God and have scriptures going into our ears regularly. Why? The answer is simple: faith comes by hearing the word of God. Indeed, the amount of technology available today leaves us with no excuse for not listening to God's word daily.

3. **SPEAK** THE WORD OF GOD
We need to keep the word of God in our mouths by regularly speaking aloud the promises of God regarding healing.

Through this daily process, I built and strengthened my foundation of faith – and I still do this as part of my everyday routine. I continue to look at, listen to, and speak the word of God each day. Take time to build your foundation! There is no faith without it!

Several years ago after moving into our present home, I noticed a house in our neighborhood that had been sitting unoccupied for a long time. The house looked good from the street, so I could not imagine what was keeping buyers from taking advantage of a quick sale. I asked various neighbors about the home, and the answer I received was always the same: *"the house has issues."* As a curious person, I wanted to know more about the specific *"issues"* present in the home. When someone finally shared with me that the house had problems with its foundation, everything began to make much more sense. Although the outside of the house appeared in good shape, the inside needed serious work. No matter how solid things looked on the surface, the foundation underneath needed significant repairs for the house to withstand the test of time.

The same can also be true with our faith foundation. On the outside, we may look like we have everything together, including our confession, a positive outlook, faithful church attendance, etc. Yet, when trouble comes, we often find that beneath the surface of our lives, the foundation of our faith is flawed. Thus, we must regularly inspect our hearts to be sure the word of God stands strong within us, not just as the rock of our salvation but also as the foundation of our faith for all we are believing God to do!

IS YOUR FOUNDATION STRONG ENOUGH TO HANDLE THE TASK?

Another point to consider is the <u>strength</u> of your faith foundation. Several years ago, Patty and I attended a conference in another state. The host church had just completed a beautiful two-story children's center. While we were there, the church's pastor shared a story with us that I will never forget. After construction began on the new building, he decided to add a third story to the project. He consulted the architect and engineers and was surprised when they informed him the addition would not be possible. The pastor's initial response was: *"It's my building. I'll do as I please."* However, the engineers explained to him that the foundation was designed only to support two floors. To build anything more than two stories would compromise the foundation and put the entire building at risk of a possible collapse. Likewise, we must plan accordingly when building our faith foundation. If our faith has barely enough strength to overcome a headache, how can we expect it to be strong enough to overcome cancer or another serious disease without collapsing? We must build a foundation of faith with enough strength to withstand ALL the enemy sends our way. The only way to do this is by spending the necessary time in God's word. There are no shortcuts to building a strong faith foundation!

CHAPTER 2

Is Healing the Will of God?

When pursuing anything from the Lord by faith, we must be convinced His will is for us to have what we seek, which is especially true concerning receiving healing by faith. As we established in the first chapter, Bible faith is not *"wishing"* something would happen, nor is it merely believing God CAN do something. Instead, biblical faith believes God WILL move – or has ALREADY moved – in our circumstances. When pursuing healing, the first question we should ask ourselves is: *"Do I fully believe*

God's will IS for me to be healed?" If the answer is *"yes,"* we should then ask ourselves: *"*WHY *do I believe this is His will?"*

KNOWING **WHAT** WE BELIEVE AND **WHY** WE BELIEVE IT ARE KEY COMPONENTS IN THE FUNCTION OF FAITH.

Because the word of God is the foundation of our faith, the answers we give to these questions must be rooted and grounded in the word. I cannot simply believe healing is mine because another person receives their healing. Likewise, I cannot base my faith on stories I hear told by my favorite television minister. Faith does not come by hearing testimonies or a good song on the radio. Although such things can serve to stir up the faith already residing within us, the foundation of true, lasting faith is <u>always</u> the word of God. My knowledge and understanding regarding God's will to heal should be based on His word, not the words or even the experiences of others.

However, what if you answered *"no"* to whether you believe God's will is to heal? What then? Because biblical faith for healing requires first believing God's will IS to heal, the next question I would suggest you ask yourself is: *"Why do I* NOT *believe healing is for me?"* Could your lack of belief stem from the traditions you grew up in or, perhaps, from listening to sermons based on people's opinions rather than God's word? No matter your background, I encourage you to continue reading this book with an open heart so that, above all else, you may receive for yourself what His word says.

THE ORIGIN OF SICKNESS

When establishing our belief that healing is for us, we must first consider the origin of sickness and disease. The Bible does not mention sickness or disease when speaking of the Garden of Eden. A thorough examination of the six days of Creation also yields no indication of what day God made cancer, diabetes, or any other disease. Why? The answer is very simple: because GOD DID NOT CREATE SICKNESS. Sickness and disease came as a result of the fall of man. After Adam and Eve sinned, all sickness, pain, sorrow, poverty, lack, worry, fear, and everything else associated with death, darkness, and the curse entered into God's creation. What caused this to happen? Although God gave His created human race a perfect environment in which to enjoy life, when Adam sinned, he gave up his God-given authority to subdue and have dominion in the earth realm. After man's fall, Satan became the god of this world. When this new leader entered the scene, he brought all that is opposite of God's character into the earth.

For example, God gave all provision to man; Satan took everything away. God brought blessing to His creation; Satan brought everything cursed into the creation. God is a good God; Satan is a bad and evil ruler. From the time of Adam's fall onward, we witness everything associated with Satan coming upon the earth. We also see the great and marvelous love of God who, in His great wisdom and mercy, had already prepared and planned for man's fall by providing a lamb – Jesus – slain from the foundation of the world. God has always been working to bring the human race back into full relationship with Him so that He can continue being a good God to His creation.

HEALING FROM THE BEGINNING

One might ask: *"What does this have to with healing?"* My answer would simply be: *"everything!"* From the beginning, when God began working with fallen man to restore the human race, He provided healing. For example, let us look at the book of Exodus, where the writer, Moses, explains how God delivered His people from Egyptian bondage. In Chapter 12, we find instructions for the first Passover, which is significant as Passover is considered a type and shadow of what would come through the body and blood of the Lord Jesus.

Later on, in Chapter 13, we read how the Israelites began their journey out of Egypt toward the land God had promised them. Most scholars believe more than two million people took part in this departure. In a group of this size, many must have experienced some type of sickness, especially considering the harsh conditions they had suffered as Egyptian slaves. Yet notice what the Psalmist says regarding the health of the Israelites who took part in the Exodus:

> *"He brought them forth also with silver and gold: and <u>there was not one feeble person among their tribes</u>."*
>
> PSALM 105:37

Here the word *"feeble"* means to stumble, stagger, or be weak. When God brought His people out of Egypt, He healed them of all weaknesses and illnesses, including those that might have hindered them in walking through the many miles of desert. God wanted His people to leave Egypt free of sickness and disease, with some translations stating He brought them forth *"healthy and strong.*" If God was so moved by the sickness of His people in Egypt that He brought them healing and deliverance from disease through the first Passover lamb, how much more healing and deliverance has He made available to us through Jesus, the Perfect Lamb?

HEALING IN THE OLD COVENANT

As we continue looking at the Bible's historical accounts of God working to bring the human race back to Himself, we see Him establishing various covenants with mankind throughout the Old Testament. Ultimately, each of these covenants point toward the final covenant God would establish with lost humanity through His own Son, Jesus. The terms *"Old Covenant"* and *"New Covenant"* are still heard often in the Church today. When speaking of the Old Covenant, most are referencing the Mosaic Covenant, which God gave to His people through Moses (Chapter 28 of the book of Deuteronomy contains an excellent overview of this covenant). The basis of the Old Covenant was the Ten

Commandments, and its nature was to provide blessings for obedience and curses for disobedience. When building our foundation for healing, we must keep in mind that, even in the Old Covenant, God explicitly provides healing and divine health for His people:

> *"...if thou wilt diligently hearken to the voice of the Lord thy God, and wilt do that which is right in his sight, and wilt give ear to his commandments, and keep all his statutes, <u>I will put none of these diseases upon thee</u>, which I have brought upon the Egyptians: for I am the Lord that healeth thee."*
>
> EXODUS 15:26

The Old Covenant included healing as a blessing, while sickness was considered a curse. Chapter 28 of the book of Deuteronomy emphasizes God's provision of healing for His people, even listing diseases as part of the curse.

As you build your faith foundation, be sure NEVER to confuse blessings with curses!

WHAT GOD CALLS A BLESSING SHOULD NEVER BE CONSIDERED A CURSE, AND WHAT HIS WORD CONSIDERS A CURSE MUST NEVER BE CALLED A BLESSING.

Some might be quick to point out how certain passages of scripture seem to indicate God sometimes *"sends"* sickness and disease upon His people. To provide better clarity, we must consider the original languages of the Bible, as well as the specific meanings of certain biblical terms. For instance, in Exodus 15:25, God speaks of not putting the diseases He brought upon the Egyptians upon His people. More specifically, the Hebrew translation of this text indicates God *"permitted"* these diseases rather than *"sent"* them. For those who may struggle with this concept, consider this point: the Old Testament saints operated within a covenant containing harsh judgment for breaking even the least of God's laws. However, we are no longer under the Old Covenant. Those of us who receive Christ are born into a NEW COVENANT – one where Jesus already took OUR harsh judgment upon Himself by way of the cross:

> "_Christ hath redeemed us from the curse of the law,_ being made a curse for us: for it is written, Cursed is every one that hangeth on a tree..."
>
> GALATIANS 3:13

I believe God's will to heal is best summed up in Exodus 15:26 when He proclaims: *"I am the Lord that _healeth thee._"* God's nature is – and always has been – to heal!

HEALING IN THE MINISTRY OF JESUS

Another avenue by which we can further strengthen our foundation of faith for healing is to look at the ministry of Jesus. As the Gospels reveal, His ministry was filled with many great healings. The Gospels record at least thirty-seven accounts of miracles, with most – but certainly not all – being related to healing the sick. Some passages of scripture even describe how Jesus healed great multitudes. As Matthew writes:

"...and Jesus went about all Galilee, teaching in their synagogues, and preaching the gospel of the kingdom, and _healing all_ _manner of sickness and all manner of disease_ among the people. And his fame went throughout all Syria: and they brought unto him _all sick people_ that were taken with divers diseases and torments, and those which were possessed with devils, and those which were lunatick, and those that had the palsy; _and he healed them_..."

MATTHEW 4:23-24

The indication in this passage is that NO ONE was left out! Yet, this is not the only instance where scripture describes Jesus as having healed ALL who were sick. For those who may still be skeptical, here are some additional examples where the word of God is very specific in stating Jesus healed everyone:

- MATTHEW 12:15
- MARK 6:56
- LUKE 4:40
- LUKE 6:19
- LUKE 9:11

WHAT IS MISSING IN THE MINISTRY OF JESUS?

Taking note of what is MISSING in Jesus' ministry to the sick is also helpful in establishing faith for healing. No account exists in either of the four gospels where Jesus denied healing to anyone - not even once. Likewise, NO record exists in scripture of Jesus ever saying to a sick person: *"you cannot be healed because it is God's will for you to remain sick"* or *"you cannot be healed because my Father is using your sickness to teach you something."* Unfortunately, even though Jesus Himself never made statements like this, preachers have told people such things for years! As a result, many people cannot have simple faith for healing because such non-biblical words ring LOUDER in their spiritual ears than the actual words of Jesus.

If using sickness as a tool was indeed God's will, I am convinced we would have a record of Jesus encountering at least one person – out of the multitudes that He met – to whom the Father taught a lesson by using disease or illness. Yet, no such record exists. How then did Jesus react to sickness? Writing in the book of Acts, Luke clearly describes how Jesus responded:

"...God anointed Jesus of Nazareth with the Holy Ghost and with power:

who went about doing good, and

healing all that were oppressed of

the devil; for God was with him."

ACTS 10:38

As this passage of scripture clearly states: Jesus HEALED ALL. Furthermore, sickness is characterized as an oppressive condition and attributed to the devil, not God.

HEALING IN THE EARLY CHURCH

Are you now beginning to see the will of God regarding sickness and disease? From the start, healing has existed. The first covenant made provision for it, and we see it present and active throughout the earthly ministry of Jesus. However, what about after the death of Jesus? Did God's will regarding healing change? No. The healing power of God is evident in some of the very first activities recorded in the early Church. In the third chapter of Acts, we find the historical account of a lame man being completely healed. A few chapters later, in Acts 5:16, we read of another event where *"everyone"* in a multitude was healed – EVERYONE!

The healing ministry of the early Church mirrored the healing ministry of Jesus from the beginning. Healing miracles occurred throughout the book of Acts because the Church's ministry was – and STILL is – intended to be a CONTINUATION of the ministry of Jesus in the earth. Contrary to the popular belief of some religious circles:

NO SCRIPTURE EXISTS TO SUPPORT ANY DOCTRINE STATING HEALINGS AND MIRACLES HAVE CEASED.

As such, healings and miracles should be just as much a part of the Church of today as they were in the early Church described in the book of Acts.

Yet, the accounts contained within the book of Acts are not the only support God's word gives for the continued ministry of healing in the Church. Look at this passage from the book of James:

"Is <u>any sick</u> among you? let him call for the elders of the church; and let them pray over him, anointing him with oil in the name of the Lord: <u>And the prayer of faith shall save the sick,</u> and the Lord shall raise him up; and if he have committed sins, they shall be forgiven him."

JAMES 5:14-15

Why would James, writing by the inspiration of the Holy Spirit, instruct the Church on matters regarding ministry to the sick if the ministry of healing was not intended to continue? Also, note these instructions contain no restrictions regarding who may or may not partake in being healed. James simply asks, *"is* ANY *among you sick?"* In addition, no mention is made regarding the Lord *"sending"* sickness as a manifestation of His will or as a way to teach someone a lesson. Again, as we discussed earlier, God does not *"send"* sickness upon anyone. His nature and will regarding disease have always been to heal! God's position on the matter has not changed and will not change, and neither should ours. The Church of today should still be ministering healing in the same way as the early Church!

CHAPTER 3

Does Faith Make a Difference?

Now that a strong case for healing has been presented, your faith should already be on the increase. However, I feel it necessary to remind you Bible faith MUST have its foundation in the word of God. Our faith will continue to grow and develop as we give time to God's word daily. Faith is vital in the life of the believer.

"But without <u>faith</u> it is impossible to please him..."

HEBREWS 11:6

The only means by which we can please God is by faith! Everything we receive from God requires faith, and faith is the key that unlocks the door to heaven's treasures. How important is faith regarding receiving healing? Extremely! In fact, throughout the ministry of Jesus, healings and miracles were often attributed to the presence of faith. In contrast, a lack of faith often hindered entire cities and villages from receiving such blessings from God.

In the Gospel of Mark, we find the account of the woman with the issue of blood. Scripture very clearly states the woman had been sick for twelve years, and her health continued to decline despite having sought the help of many doctors. To make matters worse, her medical bills had left her in financial ruin. Can you relate? Yet, by the end of Mark's account of the woman's battle with sickness, we find she was made completely whole! What changed her circumstances? What made the difference? Mark gives us insight through a very simple statement: *"When she had heard of Jesus..."* (Mark 5:27). What the woman HEARD produced faith. Then – by faith – she was able to believe if she touched the garment of Jesus, she would receive the healing her doctors had been unable to provide. What exactly did she hear that produced the faith to receive? Scripture simply tells us she heard *"of Jesus."* What sorts of things might she have heard about Him? We can assume she must have heard about the many great miracles He had performed. Maybe she heard how He healed the blind and the lame. She might have even heard He raised the dead. Regardless, whatever she heard produced great faith within her – enough faith for her to say to herself: *"if He did it for them, I believe He can do it for me."*

Several points from the woman's experience are worth noting, including what she chose to say, her willingness to act on her faith, and her persistence. However, the words of Jesus Himself reveal the greatest message of her story when He says to her: *"Daughter, thy faith hath made thee whole…"* (Mark 5:34). Faith played an important – and necessary – role in her receiving healing. Remember, too, that she was still living under the Old Covenant. The new birth was not yet available. If this woman's faith could make her whole, how much more can our faith accomplish since we have been born again and have a new covenant based on better promises than the old?

As I mentioned in the first chapter, my foundation of faith was already good when I was diagnosed with CLL in 2015. I believed healing was provided for in the atonement of Christ. I knew the importance of feeding on God's word daily, especially His healing promises. I knew from previous battles that my faith needed to develop to match the fight in which we were engaged. In writing to Timothy, the Apostle Paul refers to *"the good fight of faith"* (1 Timothy 6:12). I have heard some say: *"it's a 'good fight' because we win,"* and I do agree. However, although our victory is promised, a fight is still involved! The fight is to stay in faith throughout the process. Yes, some healings do occur instantaneously when the gifts of healing or miracles are in operation, both of which 1 Corinthians 12:9 lists as gifts of the Holy Spirit. However, other healings or miracles take place gradually. In my experience, I have found any miracle occurring progressively over time will require a faith fight. The good fight of faith involves standing by faith and staying in faith until the full manifestation of healing arrives. You might ask: *"how long do you fight?"* The answer is: as long as it takes! Faith does not concern itself with circumstances or the time required for manifestation; faith simply takes its position on the word of God and waits expectantly.

My first personal experience with faith for healing occurred early in my ministry. My jaw began locking unpredictably, causing me considerable pain and discomfort until I could maneuver it back into place. This issue continued for several months. At the time, Patty and I were doing a considerable amount of evangelistic work, as this was before we began pastoring churches. We would often leave town on Friday evening and preach in churches over the weekend, then return home late Sunday night in order to go back to work the following morning. On one particular trip, we left town on a Wednesday evening to preach in one church and were scheduled to begin revival the next evening in another.

While preaching during the Wednesday evening service, my jaw completely locked, and I was in severe pain! Being a man who is not always willing to show my weakness, I quickly diverted the attention and moved into a simple and very brief altar service. Eventually, I was able to shift my jaw back into place. The Lord then spoke to me, saying: *"have Pastor Eugene Ratliff lay hands on you and pray for you tomorrow evening, and I will heal you."* I was scheduled to be at Pastor Ratliff's church the next day. However, since my jaw was feeling normal again, and I was no longer experiencing pain, I did not give much additional thought to what the Lord had said. I preached the following evening with

NO pain and NO issues. After I closed the service and turned it back over to Pastor Ratliff, the Lord reminded me of what He had told me the night before. I now had a choice: obey God or ignore Him. Obedience is always best! I stopped Pastor Ratliff in the middle of the dismissal prayer and asked him to lay hands on me and pray for my jaw. I would love to tell you the earth shook under my feet after he prayed. However, I felt nothing! ABSOLUTELY NOTHING!

After the service, Patty and I went to Pastor Ratliff's home, where we were spending the night. Suddenly, while in the room where we were staying, my jaw locked again. Immediately I sensed the voice of the Lord speaking to me again. This time He said: *"What are you going to do now? Are you going to believe you did* NOT *receive your healing when Eugene Ratliff laid hands on you? Or are you going to believe you* DID *receive?"* That night, I decided to PLACE MY FAITH for my healing. Every time my jaw locked in the days following, I would immediately say: *"Thank you,*

Lord, that I received my healing when Eugene Ratliff laid hands on me." I cannot tell you how many times I did this, but the number was considerable. This process continued for weeks with no noticeable results in my flesh. Declaring my healing through praise whenever my jaw would lock became the norm for me. In time, the declaration of healing became more real to me than the pain in my face. Then, suddenly, one day the pain and locking jaw were gone!

That experience taught me a valuable lesson on how faith works. Faith does not move based on the circumstances. Instead, faith settles the issue based solely on the promises of God.

TO RECEIVE BY FAITH, WE MUST FIRST BELIEVE WHAT WE SEEK HAS ALREADY BEEN COMPLETED IN THE SPIRIT, EVEN BEFORE IT IS MANIFESTED IN THE NATURAL.

Simply put, I had to receive and believe my jaw was healed even BEFORE the symptoms left. Waiting until AFTER the symptoms were gone before believing would have required NO faith on my part. Once I received the manifestation of my healing, I believe God's word to me was: *"Son, thy faith hath made the whole"* – just as He had said to the woman with the issue of blood.

I have had many more opportunities to use my faith to receive healing from the Lord since the incident with my jaw. This is especially true concerning my experience with CLL. As I mentioned earlier in the book, my diagnosis came in August 2015. I had developed a swollen lymph node in my neck that my medical doctor insisted I have removed. My white blood cell count was also elevated, which was not a reason for much concern since I seemed in otherwise excellent health. I scheduled the simple surgery and went about my life as usual. I was busy pastoring our church, Grace Fellowship, in London, Kentucky, which had just entered a major transition phase. We were in the process of buying property for the church, beginning a complete renovation of the existing onsite building, and constructing a new preschool facility.

On a Wednesday morning, I received a call from my surgeon, who was also a friend and attendee of our church. He told me the diagnosis – chronic lymphocytic leukemia, or CLL – and began explaining what he knew about this type of leukemia. He instructed me to see an oncologist immediately and set up a treatment plan. Many of you might expect me to use the next several sentences to describe how great fear and anxiety arose in our hearts from this diagnosis. After all, leukemia is a type of blood cancer, the *"C word"*! Yet, I had NO PANIC upon hearing this report. Instead, I called my wife to share what the doctor had said, and we ended our conversation in agreement, not fearfulness. We both knew exactly what was needed to fight – and to win – this battle: FAITH.

By Thursday of the following week, I was in Lexington, Kentucky, seeing an oncologist. He quickly explained I had done nothing to cause this disease and that, in his words, it was simply a case of *"bad luck."* However, I do not believe in *"luck"* and especially not *"bad luck"!* The doctor continued to explain how treatment to help the condition was available, but no cure existed and, according to medical experts, I would live and eventually die with this disease. You might ask: *"were you panicking yet?"* My answer was still: *"*NO!*"* Faith and fear do not – and cannot – coexist, as one will always drive out the other. I chose to allow my faith to drive out fear. We left the meeting with a plan that included a regimen of blood tests and scans every three months to monitor the progression of the disease. The results of those tests would then determine the timing of my treatment – including possible chemotherapy.

Over the next year, nothing changed in my symptoms except an elevation of my white blood cells. Rather than publicly sharing the diagnosis and battle with our congregation, Patty and I decided to build our faith privately while standing in agreement for complete healing during this time. I was in one of the busiest times of my life as we prepared to move our entire ministry from one location to another. Although the relocation process required considerable time and labor from me, I never allowed anything to distract me from spending MUCH time in God's word. The word was – and still is – my sure foundation for building my faith and receiving victory in ALL battles!

NO WORD = NO FAITH
NO FAITH = NO VICTORY

I was convinced faith would overcome this disease. From the time I was first given the diagnosis in August 2015, I worked diligently on BUILDING my foundation of faith, and, in August 2016, I SETTLED my faith for healing. I actually made a notation in the back of my

Bible that reads: *"August 13, 2016 – I received my healing by faith!"* Nothing had changed in my physical body, but something HAD changed in my spirit. My faith level had been growing and had now reached a level where it could be released to receive the healing for which I had been believing. Faith had made a difference for me, just as it had for many individuals throughout the Bible. As scripture declares: God is no respecter of persons. If the faith of those in biblical times worked healings and miracles for them, my faith would do the same for me. Yes, faith DOES make a difference!

CHAPTER 4

Help, My Faith Isn't Working!

I would love to begin this chapter by being able to say my faith immediately produced results in my health and all signs of CLL disappeared once I received my healing by faith. However, this was NOT exactly the way things worked. By December 2016, we were on schedule to relocate the entire ministry to the new location. Our old facility needed to be vacated by no later than the last day of 2016, so the move could not be delayed. I had begun noticing changes in my energy levels during this time, but I pressed through.

On January 1, 2017, we held our first service in the new building. This was an exciting time! Grace Fellowship finally had its own property after leasing facilities for ten years. I was preaching during every service, but I had started to experience some shortness of breath. My office was located on the upper level of our new facility, and reaching it required my climbing several flights of stairs. Often, I would be entirely out of breath by the time I reached the top. Another clue something was not quite right occurred while I was attending one of my son's ballgames and I began feeling so light-headed I had to leave the gym. I was so dizzy that I barely made it outside to sit on the curb and nearly passed out. However, I simply thought the crowd and stuffy atmosphere were to blame.

Being stubborn, I did not go to the doctor or the emergency room. By this time, I had also stopped seeing my oncologist. During my final visit with him, he indicated the disease had now reached Stage IV, yet he gave me no plan for treatment. He was always negative, never positive, and I felt in my spirit that he was not offering me much help. Indeed, one thing I have learned during my healing journey is that following the Holy Spirit's lead in <u>all</u> things – including your choice of doctors – is very important.

WHEN BELIEVING FOR HEALING, ALLOWING THE HOLY SPIRIT TO LEAD YOU TO THE **RIGHT** MEDICAL PROFESSIONALS IS ESSENTIAL.

I felt certain the Holy Spirit had led me to <u>leave</u> the care of that particular doctor, and I was just as certain HE would lead me <u>to</u> the *right* doctor in His perfect time. In fact, when these new symptoms began to manifest, I already had an appointment scheduled with a new medical doctor with whom God had connected me. My goal was to wait until this appointment and allow Him to direct me to a new oncologist before seeking any additional treatment. What I did not know at the time was that the disease had taken an extremely aggressive turn, and I was actually in great danger of experiencing a heart attack.

On February 9, 2017, I went to see my regular family physician. Because of the new issues I had recently developed with my health, he ordered lab work before the appointment and had the results sent to his office ahead of my visit. When my doctor entered the exam room that day, he immediately told me my hemoglobin was in the 4's, which is an extremely dangerous level (a normal hemoglobin level is 12.5 to 13 or above). I would need a blood transfusion as soon as possible. He was amazed I could get around so well and even more surprised when I told him I had driven myself to his office. At this point in the battle, things with my health began to change drastically and quickly, starting with my spending the night in the hospital receiving an emergency blood transfusion. On a humorous note, up until this point, I had not known my blood type. While at the hospital, one of the nurses came in and told me my blood type was B+. My response to her was: *"I knew it would 'BE' positive!"* They successfully raised my hemoglobin level to almost 6 before releasing me, but in the meantime my white blood cell count (WBC) had gone through the roof. A normal WBC range is around 3,500 to 10,500 cells/mcL, but mine was at 160,000! I needed a manifestation of healing or some type of treatment – and quickly! The issues in my health simply could not continue as they were.

The week following the blood transfusion, I met with the new oncologist I believed God would use to aid in healing my body. I had already sensed in my spirit that God wanted me to work with this particular doctor. When we met for the first time, I immediately knew I had been right about him – God would use this man as an instrument in my healing. I must say something very important here:

> AT TIMES GOD HEALS INSTANTANEOUSLY THROUGH **SUPERNATURAL** MEANS; SOMETIMES, HE HEALS THROUGH A **PROGRESSIVE** WORK; AND AT OTHER TIMES, HE HEALS BY WORKING **WITH AND THROUGH** MEDICAL SCIENCE.

From the first appointment, this new oncologist was extremely positive, despite my deteriorating condition. He ordered additional, immediate testing, including scans, labs, and a bone marrow biopsy. The tests verified the doctor's theory: leukemia had taken over my bone marrow to the point my body could no longer produce blood. Also, although CLL usually is not very aggressive, my genetics had caused the disease to take on an extremely aggressive form in my body. The recommended treatment was immediate chemotherapy for the next six months. Our response to my doctor was simple: *"We are people of faith. You do what YOU do, we will do what WE do, and God will do what HE does!"*

Many people might have given up their faith fight at this point. However, this is why reminding ourselves repeatedly that faith is NOT moved by circumstances is so important. Bible faith is founded on the word of God. Circumstances may change, but God's word does not. Therefore, the position of our faith does not change simply because of adverse situations. Initially, Patty and I believed for complete healing without any treatment, especially chemotherapy. Yet, when the disease worsened, and I was confronted with the treatment options, I had to make a serious decision. Would I consent to a type of treatment I had watched others struggle with or even die from? What was the best course of action? When faced with this type of situation, you MUST allow the

Holy Spirit to guide you in your decisions. I felt God had directed me to my present physician and that I was supposed to follow my doctor's guidance in treatment. Thus, we decided to begin the recommended treatment, placing our faith on the medications to work ONLY to my benefit. We specifically believed by faith that I would only receive the BEST from the treatments, with no side effects to work against my health.

I remember the first day of chemotherapy very well. Before even starting the treatment, Patty and I had to first sit through over an hour of instruction regarding the potentially harmful side effects the chemo drugs could – and most likely would – have on my body. The list was EXTENSIVE and included symptoms such as nausea, diarrhea, vomiting, weakness, pain, hair loss, mouth blisters, and much more. The nurse instructing us was very kind, and Patty and I quietly listened as she spoke. However, once she finished going over all the information, I felt compelled in my spirit to say to her:

"thank you, but we are people of faith, and we are not anticipating any of this." She looked at me like I had just arrived from another planet! Yet, within a few weeks, she was amazed at how well I was doing. I ended up only having very minor side effects from the chemo.

Along with chemotherapy, I was also taking very high doses of steroids. However, I did not realize these meds, like the chemo, also had potentially serious side effects, and I was not as adamant about using my faith while taking them. As a result, I experienced a major reaction to the steroids learning the important lesson of using your faith with ALL medications! My initial chemotherapy plan was three days per month for six months. After completing my second month of treatment, friends and family members were astonished the chemo had not caused any real hindrances to my daily routine. I was still preaching in every service, enjoying life, and doing nearly everything I desired.

However, by the third month of treatment, my situation had so drastically changed that my third round of chemo was the last! I began experiencing chills and shakes. Despite taking various antibiotics and an extreme dosage of steroids, I also developed a low-grade fever that would not break. My doctor could find no solid explanation for why I was having such strange symptoms. He speculated I may have experienced a reaction to one of the treatment meds, but to this day, I still do not have a full answer as to what happened.

I chilled no matter where I went and became so weak that I could barely get dressed in the morning. My days consisted of forcing myself out of bed, making the dreaded trip down the stairs, and finally coming to rest on the living room sofa. I lost my appetite and was losing weight at a considerable rate. I also developed a severe cough that prompted my being referred to another doctor specializing in lung treatment. The trips to my doctors' appointments became miserable, and I came to truly understand the statement: *"I'm too sick to go to the doctor."* I made twice-weekly trips to LabCorp, an outpatient facility in London, to have lab work done. Then the results were sent immediately to my oncologist in Lexington to see if I needed a blood transfusion. For several weeks, my wife and I would go to have my labs drawn and then wait until we received a call back regarding my results. More often than not, we would then immediately make an hour-long trip to Lexington for blood typing, only to make the same trip to Lexington again the following day so I could receive blood. The employees at LabCorp considered me their most serious case and, thankfully, allowed me to bypass the usual lines and receive immediate care, as they knew I was too weak to wait. One of their workers later shared with me that I became a priority because my physical condition had deteriorated to the point I looked, in her words, as though I was *"knocking on heaven's door."*

During this time, Patty worked at the church office on weekdays and covered Sunday services for me as needed. On several occasions, I found myself at home alone, and this was when the REAL tests came – not just physically but mentally as well. Would I change my mind regarding what faith could do? Or would I stand on the word of God and hold tight to my confession of healing? At my weakest point, I did not feel like doing much at all, even concerning my faith fight. However, I was still determined not to give up, even if I only had enough strength to simply declare: *"my confession is still: I am healed by the stripes of Jesus."* My faith may not have seemed like it was working, but I refused to change my confession!

Remember, Bible faith does not rest on outward circumstances. Bible faith is based entirely upon the word of God. Sometimes, when faith does not seem like it is working is when it is actually at its best! Although nothing was yet visible in the natural, MY FAITH WAS WORKING!

CHAPTER 5

Faith Speaks: What Is Your Faith Saying?

Throughout my healing journey, the Holy Spirit became more real to me as both Teacher and Guide. I often felt Him prompt me to do certain things, some of which were more familiar to me than others. One thing is for certain: when confronted with a life-or-death battle, I became willing to follow the Spirit's leading in all things. This willingness to follow His lead included my allowing Him to direct me regarding what words I should speak during the fight! Indeed, several years even before the CLL diagnosis, the Lord dealt with Patty and me about the importance of speaking faith-filled words. I stand amazed at the negative words that often proceed from the mouths of many church attendees. I have witnessed people come to the altar and pray for God to move in a particular matter, only to see (and hear) them return to their seats speaking words of doubt regarding what they just requested. To me, this is a sure sign of little or no TRUE faith being exercised, despite having spent much time in prayer at the altar asking God to move.

God taught us much regarding how faith speaks during my battle with leukemia. However, before I share some of my experiences with speaking faith-filled words, let us first look at what God's word says on the subject. Sadly, many in the Church have adopted the philosophy and mindset that words do not have any power. Several years ago, while preaching on the subject of *"words matter,"* I remember a woman in the congregation who very adamantly told me: *"I don't believe it makes any difference how we talk."* Regardless of how many scriptures I shared with her pointing to the opposite, her response remained the same. Rather than embracing the truth as shown in God's word, she chose to cling to what she had been taught by tradition. When seeking God's will on any subject, I encourage you to FIRST go to His word.

BE SURE YOUR BELIEFS – AND BELIEF SYSTEM – ARE FOUNDED ON WHAT <u>SCRIPTURE</u> SAYS AND **NOT** BASED SIMPLY ON LONGSTANDING CHURCH OR FAMILY <u>TRADITIONS</u>.

Contrary to what many believe, God's word has MUCH to say about the power of words! Here are a few of my favorite passages on the power of what we speak:

"Death and life are in the power of the tongue: and they that love it shall eat the fruit thereof."

PROVERBS 18:21

*"For by thy words thou shalt
be justified, and by thy words
thou shalt be condemned."*

MATTHEW 12:37

*"O generation of vipers, how can ye,
being evil, speak good things? for out of
the abundance of the heart the mouth
speaketh. A good man out of the good
treasure of the heart bringeth forth
good things: and an evil man out of the
evil treasure bringeth forth evil things."*

MATTHEW 12:34-35

*"A man shall eat good by the fruit
of his mouth: but the soul of the
transgressors shall eat violence. He
that keepeth his mouth keepeth
his life: but he that openeth wide
his lips shall have destruction."*

PROVERBS 13:2-3

If you still struggle with understanding God's view regarding the power of words, I encourage you to do a study on your own. You will find the Bible is filled with many great passages on this subject. Two scriptures, in particular, changed our lives regarding how Patty and I viewed the power of our words. The first is a very well-known passage found in the book of Mark:

"For verily I say unto you, That whosoever shall say unto this mountain, Be thou removed, and be thou cast into the sea; and shall not doubt in his heart, but shall believe that those things which he saith shall come to pass; he shall have whatsoever he saith. Therefore I say unto you, What things soever ye desire, when ye pray, believe that ye receive them, and ye shall have them."

MARK 11:23-24

Note this scripture's emphasis on the actual act of SAYING things to our mountains. I often find people who only pray about the difficulties in their lives or, more specifically, pray for God to remove them. However, scripture teaches us not only to pray about our mountains but also to SPEAK to them directly!

THERE ARE TIMES WHEN WE SHOULD **PRAY** AND TIMES WHEN WE SHOULD **SPEAK**!

The second passage of scripture that helped us recognize the power of our words is in Chapter 3 of the book of Acts. Recorded here is the first healing miracle to occur in the newly birthed Church: the healing of a lame man at the temple. In the account, Peter and John encounter this man – who had been lame since birth – as he is begging for alms at the temple entrance:

*"Then Peter said, Silver and gold
have I none; but such as I have give
I thee: In the name of Jesus Christ of
Nazareth rise up and walk. And he
took him by the right hand, and lifted
him up: and immediately his feet and
ankle bones received strength."*

ACTS 3:6-7

As this passage points out, Peter SPOKE to the man's condition rather than praying for him. While praying at all times is essential, we must also be willing to SPEAK as the Holy Spirit directs us. If placed in the same situation as Peter, I believe most of today's ministers would choose to simply pray for the lame man's healing rather than speak in authority to his condition.

Again, take note of the earlier passage where Jesus clearly states if we believe what we say will come to pass, we will have the things we say! How I thought about my words changed when I discovered this scripture. Why?

Because if I truly believe what I am saying can come to pass, I will choose my words very wisely! I realize tradition causes some to struggle with this teaching. However, let me remind you Who spoke about this principle in scripture: JESUS HIMSELF!

The book of James contains another great passage about words:

> "*For in many things we offend all. If any man offend not in word, the same is a perfect man, and able also to bridle the whole body. Behold, we put bits in the horses' mouths, that they may obey us; and we turn about their whole body. Behold also the ships, which though they be so great, and are driven of fierce winds, yet are they turned about with a very small helm, whithersoever the governor listeth.*"

JAMES 3:2-4

The basic message James wants us to understand concerning the tongue is simple: OUR WORDS DIRECT OUR LIVES. Just as a bridle dictates the direction a horse travels, our tongue sets the direction for our life. The same is true for the rudder of a ship. Although small compared to the great vessel it steers, the rudder is still crucial in setting – and maintaining – the ship's direction. Remember, just as a ship follows the course set by its rudder, our lives follow our thoughts and words. Thus, we can rise no higher than our thinking or speaking allows.

You may ask: *"what does this have to do with healing?"* The answer is everything! Using faith effectively for healing requires the use of our words, as words are the expression of our faith.

FAITH IS VOICE ACTIVATED:
NO FAITH WORDS =
NO ACTIVE FAITH!

Most Christians can comprehend the connection between our faith and our words when applied to the basics of salvation. From a very early age, I learned that to be saved, I had to believe with my heart and confess with my mouth. I often joke how all those raised in the Baptist faith – like me – can quote by heart the *"Romans Road of Salvation,"* which says in part:

> *"That if thou shalt confess with thy mouth the Lord Jesus, and shalt believe in thine heart that God hath raised him from the dead, thou shalt be saved. For with the heart man believeth unto righteousness; and with the mouth confession is made unto salvation."*
>
> ROMANS 10:9-10

In fact, the church in which I grew up required a newly saved person to give a public confession immediately after praying the sinner's prayer. In regard to receiving salvation, we clearly understood the significance of and the requirement for CONFESSION / PROFESSION. Yet, despite understanding how the process of combining faith with one's words worked for salvation, that church, like many others, never seemed to grasp how the same process worked in receiving anything more. Regardless of the biblical promise for which one is believing, be it salvation, healing, or something else, faith and confession go together. One without the other is useless.

When I began my faith fight for healing, I immediately started using my words. I would read aloud the healing promises found in God's word daily, sometimes even several times a day. I discovered speaking God's word out loud released a great sense of His power. At times, the Holy Spirit would also prompt me to speak specific things aloud. Sometimes He would simply have me say healing scriptures. For instance, during one of my trips to Lexington to receive blood, I specifically recall God repeatedly dealing with me to speak His word along the way. I also remember many nights when God would wake me up and prompt me to SAY things out loud. Most times, I would simply open my mouth, say whatever He had brought to my mind, and then go right back to sleep.

However, one night I recall getting out of bed to go to the bathroom and having a powerful sense of God wanting me to speak something. I opened my mouth and began to say aloud: *"I believe, therefore have I spoken. I believe; therefore, I speak."* Then I declared: *"I believe I am healed; therefore, I say I am healed!"* At the time, I did not realize a portion of my confession was actually a paraphrase of a verse of scripture: *"We having the same spirit of faith, according as it is written, I believed, and therefore have I spoken; we also believe, and therefore speak..."* (2 Corinthians 4:13). Amazingly, I did not know the location of this passage when the Spirit prompted me to speak it! I was simply exercising my faith and allowing my words to follow His lead.

Many of us grew up hearing the great historical account of how David defeated the giant, Goliath, using only a sling and a stone. Yet what we often forget is how David used strong words of faith to declare his victory over Goliath before the stone even left the sling:

"David said moreover, The Lord that delivered me out of the paw of the lion, and out of the paw of the bear, he will deliver me out of the hand of this Philistine. And Saul said unto David, Go, and the Lord be with thee."

1 SAMUEL 17:37

David believed and spoke his victory before his triumph over Goliath ever manifested. I believe this is what the Lord had me do the night I declared: *"I believe, and I speak."* As the examples in scripture repeatedly show, words are powerful. Faith is not silent; FAITH SPEAKS!

In addition to prompting me to speak scriptures, the Holy Spirit would sometimes lead me to speak <u>differently</u> than those around me. In fact, one reason Patty and I hesitated to initially share my diagnosis was to avoid others' negative talk. Far too much negativity exists in the body of Christ. We say we are praying one way, but our words go in an entirely different direction. Let me make this very clear: the prayer of faith and words of doubt, fear, unbelief, and despair are like oil and water – they do not mix. You cannot expect good results in your faith fight when combining the two.

YOU CANNOT SPEAK WORDS OF DOUBT, FEAR, UNBELIEF, AND DESPAIR ALONGSIDE THE PRAYER OF FAITH AND STILL EXPECT TO GET RESULTS!

If this is your situation, you have not taken the time necessary to build faith in your heart. God's word tells us our mouths speak out of the abundance of our hearts. When your faith level rises to a working level in your heart, your mouth will be in agreement!

I did not share my diagnosis with everyone because I knew many would react with negativity and pessimism. Even after we finally revealed our circumstances to others, we were on guard to appropriately deal with any negative words. Some people would immediately say: *"I'm so sorry,"* as if I were without any hope. Others might not say a word, but their facial expressions would speak volumes! When I was in the presence of those whose words were more doubt-filled than faith-filled, I often heard the Holy Spirit's prompting to speak something contrary to what they had said. At times, I also felt led to react similarly when interacting with my doctors or nurses. Although they might make a factual statement in the natural regarding my situation, I would feel led to speak up and counter those FACTS with the TRUTH from God's word. One very important lesson I learned during this time was always to be willing to speak up and speak out regarding what GOD says. This is how faith is released!

Faith-filled words contain great power; like David, my words of faith were bringing down the giant of leukemia! Jesus said He would only say what He heard the Father say, and He also taught how the Holy Spirit would give us words to speak. Through the prompting of the Holy Spirit, I believe God gave me words of faith to declare during my battle – and those words made a tremendous difference in my outcome!

CHAPTER 6

FAITH THAT ACTS
RECEIVES THE PRIZE

The previous chapter discussed at length the power of faith-filled words. We will now take a step further in building our faith for healing by examining the importance of ACTING on the words we speak in faith. As James 2:17 declares: *"Faith without works is dead."* Faith always demands a corresponding action. Despite having a great deal of what I refer to as *"head knowledge"* faith, some people cannot receive what they know to be true simply because their level of faith is not great enough to prompt them into action. These individuals believe the word of God, but not strongly enough to walk in it. Take, for example, the people of Israel as they pursued the Promised Land. They had heard the promises of God regarding this great place and witnessed many great miracles as He led them on their journey. As a result, their faith grew to a certain level. However, when the time came for Israel to put their faith into ACTION, it was not developed enough to step into the land God had already assured them was theirs.

SIMPLY SAYING, "**I HAVE FAITH**," IS NOT ENOUGH. YOU MUST HAVE FAITH THAT IS DEMONSTRATED THROUGH **ACTION**!

Contrast the Israelites' lack of action in receiving the Promised Land to when David declared out loud to all of Israel that he would kill Goliath. Both the Israelites and David had faith. But only when David STEPPED OUT (the corresponding action to his words of faith) and faced the giant did he attain the victory. Talk comes easy! Talking faith is not difficult when there is no giant. Saying *"I have faith"* is easy, so long as one never needs to use that faith. However, true biblical faith – the type that gets results – does not merely speak; it is also willing to ACT!

At various points during my battle with leukemia I was required to act upon my faith. The greatest test came during a period of physical weakness, the likes of which I had never encountered before. As I mentioned earlier in the book, I experienced an unexplainable loss of strength a few months into chemotherapy, the effects of which continued for several months. During this time, even rising from my bed in the mornings to make my way downstairs to the living room sofa took incredible effort. I was so weak that just getting up to go to the restroom became a great struggle. I lost my appetite completely and was essentially force-feeding myself, and my weight quickly dropped from around 180 pounds down into the 140s. I also developed a mysterious lung condition and an intense cough. My voice weakened to a whisper. I began to understand the meaning of the saying: *"I'm too sick to go to the doctor,"* as visits to the physician's office became a dreaded experience. Although I had ministered in the past to people experiencing sickness, personally walking through a health-related battle gave me an even greater understanding of the challenges faced by others. As the weakness continued, Patty began covering all the ministerial duties at the church, including speaking during each service. On a humorous note, the church actually GREW while I was out – something I am sure any pastor would find encouraging!

A TURNING POINT

After missing three weeks of services, I was more than ready to get back to the church! Patty always encouraged me to consider attending, and I remember the weekend

I made my first attempt at returning. Patty left early for the church that Sunday morning, and my daughter, Mikaela, planned to pick me up from home in time for service. I remember attempting to get myself dressed but, try as I might, I eventually conceded my return would not happen that day. At that point, giving up might have felt like the easier choice. After all, many people do simply choose to lie down and quit when sickness comes. After my own experience, I can certainly understand how someone might succumb to such pressure. However, giving up is not a viable option when fighting a faith battle! Despite the outward circumstances or how we might *"feel"* at a given moment, Bible faith KEEPS BELIEVING!

The following Sunday, I made another attempt – and that attempt was a success! I was finally able to get dressed and make it to church. That first service back was certainly an unusual experience for me. When we arrived, my daughter pulled the car as close as possible to the side entrance. Once the service started, an associate accompanied me to my usual seat, as I was still so weak that I needed an escort to ensure I did not lose my balance and fall. I did not say anything or participate at all during the service. I would love to tell you I thoroughly enjoyed my first service back but, to be honest, I was miserable. The air conditioning was aimed directly at me, and I froze the entire time. To make matters worse, the minister (my wife, Patty) was particularly long-winded that day!

I was never so glad to leave a service as I was that morning. So, as soon as the opportunity arose, my escort led me out of the building. Some might say I should not have put myself through such an experience considering my weakened physical state at the time. However, they would be wrong! I needed to go beyond simply declaring my faith and put that faith into ACTION. Furthermore, getting dressed and coming to the service that morning was more than just a tangible ACT of my faith. I was also making a statement in the face of my enemy that boldly said: *"I refuse to quit!"*

The following week I was successful again. In addition to attending the service, I decided to add more action to my faith this time by greeting the congregation that morning. My weakened state made climbing the steps up to the platform nearly impossible for me, so Patty asked some of the men to move the podium to the floor. Little did I know then, but that particular Sunday would be a significant turning point in my health. Concerned about falling, I quietly said to my wife, *"stay close to me,"* as I approached the podium. The weakness and lung condition had greatly diminished my voice to just barely above a whisper. Some said I sounded like a ninety-year-old man.

However, when I took the mic and opened my mouth to speak, instead of a frail whisper, out came a booming voice declaring: *"praise the Lord!"* This was an amazing experience! From that moment forward my situation began to change noticeably. Since then, I have often wondered what might have happened had I NOT chosen to put my faith into action that Sunday. What if I had simply decided to stay at home on the couch? Although I do not have the answer to that question, I can confidently say the manifestation of my miracle began as I ACTED on my faith! Just two short weeks after that momentous Sunday, I was back in the pulpit full-time – and have been there ever since.

My experience should not be surprising! The Bible contains numerous examples of those who ACTED on their faith. One of my favorite healings in the ministry of Jesus was the woman with the issue of blood. She was weak. She had been sick for years. She had suffered from various treatments. Yet she refused to allow any of those things to get in the way of her receiving her miracle. Despite how she felt and how large the crowds were, and even though – according to ceremonial law – she was forbidden from being in public, the woman decided to pursue Jesus. The woman's efforts are what we call FAITH IN ACTION or faith's *"corresponding action"*! In the end, she received her miracle. Even Jesus noted how the woman's faith was the catalyst for her healing. Scripture is full of examples of others who exercised ACTIVE faith to receive from God. Indeed, as the writer of Hebrews declares:

"But without faith it is impossible to please him: for he that cometh to God must believe that he is, and that he is a rewarder of them that diligently seek him."

HEBREWS 11:6

Faith that ACTS always gets the prize!

PHOTOS

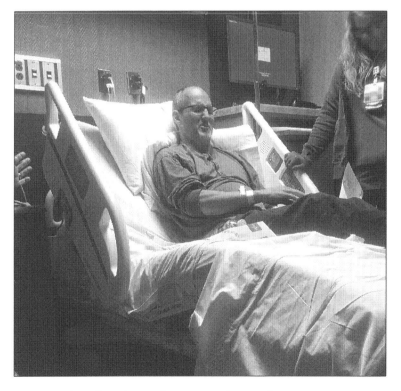

Laying hands on and praying over the very first blood transfusion Pastor Dale received in February 2017.

*Pastor Dale receives a visit from his son,
Zachary, during one of his chemo treatments.*

Pastor Dale's desk at Grace Fellowship is covered by his handwritten notes as he studies the Word and fights the good fight of faith against leukemia.

Pastor Dale studies the word alongside his wife, Patty, during one of his chemo treatments.

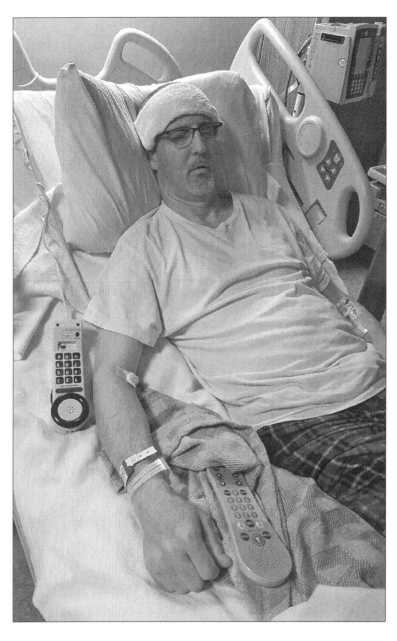

Waiting for blood before Pastor Dale's first emergency transfusion.

Even bouts of extreme weakness could not keep him from ministering. Pastor Dale teaches while seated during Sunday evening service, March 12, 2017.

Pastor Dale rests and studies his Bible during his last chemo treatment, three months sooner than doctors expected due to an intense and unexplained negative reaction. Note that the bright light seen in the doorway in the top picture cannot be fully explained. The hallway beyond has no light sources other than the ceiling fixtures shown in the lower photo, and the two shots were taken within moments of each other. Despite being one of the worst days Pastor Dale experienced during his battle, just a few weeks later he was back in the pulpit preaching full time.

Pastor Dale outside the oncology office after receiving the "all clear" report on August 20, 2017. His doctor told him: "Whatever you're doing, keep doing it!"

CHAPTER 7

The Obedience Factor

The previous chapters alluded to the importance of obedience. Regarding spiritual matters, obedience always plays a vital role. However, being obedient is more than following a set of rules or guidelines. In the New Testament Church, obedience includes following both scriptural instruction AND the Holy Spirit's directives. According to several passages of scripture, the Holy Spirit functions as both our teacher and guide:

"Howbeit when he, the Spirit of truth, is come, he will guide you into all truth: for he shall not speak of himself; but whatsoever he shall hear, that shall he speak: and he will shew you things to come."

JOHN 16:13

"But the Comforter, which is the Holy Ghost, whom the Father will send in my name, he shall teach you all things, and bring all things to your remembrance, whatsoever I have said unto you."

JOHN 14:26

Thus, when engaged in any type of spiritual fight, we should always seek the direction of the Holy Spirit regarding our battle plan. He can show us exactly what we need to do to win the war, and our position needs to be one of obedience to His specific instruction! During my healing warfare, I learned to lean heavily on the voice of the Spirit to show me what I needed to do.

Earlier in the book, I discussed how the Holy Spirit would impress upon me at times to say particular words or scriptures aloud. In addition to my speech, the Spirit guided me in other strategic ways during my time of warfare. One area where the Spirit gave me specific direction was regarding the issue of latent unforgiveness. I did not necessarily *"feel"* unforgiving toward anyone. However, the Lord knows our hearts, and at certain times the Holy Spirit would bring to my attention people or situations in my life where I needed to address unforgiveness. Unfortunately, unforgiveness is a significant problem within the Body of Christ. No greater issue has taken more people out of the local church than unforgiveness. Consider the following words of Jesus:

"For verily I say unto you, That whosoever shall say unto this mountain, Be thou removed, and be thou cast into the sea; and shall

*not doubt in his heart, but shall believe that those things which he saith shall come to pass; he shall have whatsoever he saith. Therefore I say unto you, What things soever ye desire, when ye pray, believe that ye receive them, and ye shall have them. <u>And when ye stand praying, **forgive**, if ye have ought against any: that your Father also which is in heaven **may forgive you** your trespasses.</u>"*

MARK 11:23-25

These verses relay a direct command from Jesus, and He did not leave any room for negotiation on this point. In addressing how to receive answers to our prayers, Jesus said we can speak to mountains and have the things we say if we simply believe. However, He also placed a very specific condition on the effectiveness of our *"believing and speaking"* – FORGIVENESS!

As the Lord began showing me areas and relationships in my life where unforgiveness was at work, my response was very simple: *"I forgive."* I was determined to do everything I could to OBEY every directive from the Holy Spirit. Sometimes, even when I was simply driving down the road, the Lord might bring a name to my attention, and I would say aloud, *"I forgive _____."* At other times, the Lord might lead me to bless a person – even individuals who had done me wrong in the past. Yet my reaction remained the same: *"Yes, Lord, whatever YOU say."* At other times the Holy Spirit would direct me to pray for specific people, and again my response was always one of COMPLETE OBEDIENCE.

WHILE WE SHOULD ALWAYS STRIVE TO LIVE A LIFE OF OBEDIENCE, WHEN FACED WITH A LIFE AND DEATH BATTLE, MAKE THE EFFORT TO GO THE EXTRA MILE.

Following the Spirit's guidance when choosing doctors and medical treatments is another area where obedience is crucially important during a fight for healing. I am fully convinced God directed me to the oncologist with whom I still work to this day. As I look back on the days immediately following my diagnosis, I am reminded of how the first oncologist who treated me did not sit well with my spirit. On the other hand, I remember feeling a great sense of peace when I met my present doctor. Scripture contains many instances where the early Church took similar notice of the leading of the Holy Spirit within them (for example, see Acts 15:28). Over time, I learned to follow this directive of peace from the Spirit when making decisions about my plan of care.

I also paid attention to what the Spirit said to me during discussions regarding my treatment options. For the most part, I was in full agreement with my doctor. However, I recall one occasion when I could not come to peace with a particular type of pharmaceutical treatment. Although

I did take the first injection, I refused to receive any additional doses. When I shared with my doctor that I was not at peace with taking this specific medication, he simply waived the treatment without pressuring me to continue. This is the kind of doctor you need: one who works with you and respects your opinion!

I remember another occasion when I refused a particular medical procedure. As you may recall from the previous chapter, I also developed a serious, somewhat strange lung condition during my battle with leukemia. This condition prompted my oncologist to refer me to a lung specialist, who then recommended performing a biopsy of a spot on my lung. The procedure consisted of removing and testing a small piece of my lung tissue, which carried several potential risks, including a collapsed lung. However, I was not at peace with having the biopsy. Instead, I agreed to do a less invasive procedure known as a bronchoscopy, which would allow them to examine my lungs without surgery. Interestingly, after performing the procedure, the specialist said to my wife: *"I don't know when I have seen lungs in such great shape."* Since then, I have not needed to see him again. If you want further evidence of just how complete the healing of my lungs is, visit our church and hear me preach some time!

Staying focused on hearing from the Lord and following His direction is extremely important throughout the treatment process. Remember, too, that while the Lord may often tell us things we SHOULD do, sometimes He tells us things we SHOULD NOT do. For instance, if you have lung disease due to smoking, the possibility of His leading you to quit smoking is relatively high. In such a case, your healing would be contingent upon obedience to His command. The gospel of John provides further insight into this. Here, John records the healing of a man who had been lame for thirty-eight years. After healing him, Jesus issues the man a strong command. John writes:

"Afterward Jesus findeth him [the man] in the temple, and said unto him, 'Behold, thou art made whole: sin no more, <u>lest a worse thing come unto thee</u>'."

JOHN 5:14

I do not believe personal sin is the cause of every sickness, but the possibility of sin opening a doorway to disease DOES exist. In the case of the man healed in the fifth chapter of John, sin may have opened the door to his sickness, and Jesus wanted to make sure the man kept the door closed. Jesus also indicated that by continuing in sin, the man was at risk of having an even worse thing come upon him.

WE MUST TAKE HEED OF WHAT THE HOLY SPIRIT TELLS US **TO** DO AND **NOT** TO DO.

As part of my healing battle, I had to become willing to hear – and act upon – whatever the Lord said to me. At times, this meant cutting off all secular media. At other times, the Spirit would impress upon me to adjust my diet, in particular regarding my intake of sugar. God knows if something you are eating is causing sickness in your body. He also knows if a specific action or habit in your life is potentially opening the door to the enemies of sickness and disease. As part of your pathway to healing, the Holy Spirit may reveal particular things to you. Once He has spoken, your responsibility is to heed His instruction. My advice is: ALWAYS BE QUICK TO OBEY! Your healing may be contingent upon your taking specific actions. Be quick to obey and close the door on disease once and for all.

CHAPTER 8

Go Ahead and Take It!

Now that I am in my fifties, I can look back over my life and see the various lessons I have learned so far during my time on this earth. I was taken to church for the first time not long after my birth and received salvation at eight, so I have been in church since the very beginning. Throughout my spiritual journey, God has given me instruction on many subjects, and He has spent considerable time teaching me about two in particular: faith and healing. Sadly, I have discovered the Church has many misconceptions regarding both. Often, we simply TELL people to *"have faith"* without giving INSTRUCTION on how to have it or DEMONSTRATING how to use it in everyday life. Even less instruction – and even more misunderstanding – exists in the Body of Christ regarding the subject of healing. I do not recall a single message on the topic of healing ever being preached in the denominational church of my youth. I did, however, discover a much greater emphasis on the supernatural, specifically on healing, when I came over into Pentecostal circles as a young man. However, after thirty-five years of ministry, I have witnessed a major decline in healing services and sermons on the topic, even within the Pentecostal denominations.

THE PRAYER OF FAITH

The modern Church often struggles with the concept of receiving anything from the Lord, not just healing. Many churches spend most of their time "begging"

God to move. Asking God to do specific things is not necessarily wrong, especially since the Bible contains numerous passages instructing us to ASK. However, we must do our asking within the instructional guidelines revealed in scripture.

For instance, we are quick to quote James 5:14, which speaks of "anointing the sick with oil." However, we often fail to see – and understand – a crucial component of that process found in the very next verse, which reads: "And the prayer of faith shall save the sick" (James 5:15). Although we may practice all kinds of prayer, to be effective those prayers must contain a key element: faith! When asking the Lord for specific things, we must always ask in faith. I do not believe in "begging" God for anything.

EFFECTIVE PRAYER APPROACHES GOD IN A **RECEPTIVE** MANNER.

Rather than pleading for God to move, the process of faith means we simply RECEIVE what He has already provided. For example, at salvation, I simply received Jesus into my heart by faith. I understood salvation was a gift made accessible to mankind through the Lord's finished work at the cross. Asking Him to be my Savior was not done in the sense of begging for salvation; instead, it was done as a means of ACCEPTING what Jesus had already made available to me. Receiving by faith ALL God has provided to us becomes much easier when we know and understand what His word says on a given subject.

CONFIDENCE IN KNOWING THE WILL OF GOD

Sadly, many people lack a sense of assurance that their prayers are being answered, even those who pray regularly. However, God's word declares:

"And this is the confidence that we have in him, that, if we ask any thing according to his will, he heareth us: And if we know that he hears us, whatsoever we ask, we know that we have the petitions that we desired of him."

1 JOHN 5:14-15

First, observe how this passage asserts we can have CONFIDENCE when we pray. Secondly, notice the basis of this confidence is the fact we are praying ACCORDING TO HIS WILL. Unfortunately, many believers struggle with knowing God's will. They often say, *"If I knew His will, then I could have confidence. But how do I know His will?"* What the vast majority in the Body of Christ has yet to recognize or understand is that God's WORD is His WILL!

My prayer life entirely changed once I understood that God's perfect will is revealed to me by the promises I read in His word. Now I seldom ask the Lord to do anything unless I have first opened my Bible and found a provision in His word for whatever I am asking. Once I have a promise upon which to base my request, I can pray with CONFIDENCE! I believe if God's word SAYS I can have it, then His WILL is for me to receive it. No more questioning, reasoning, or doubt. I simply take what He has already said is mine – and the enemy cannot keep it from me!

Also important to note here is that, in most every situation, God is not responsible for WITHHOLDING anything from us when we pray. Instead, He MAKES AVAILABLE to us what He has already promised in His word. God has made provision for everything I will ever need, including healing. God is not trying to *"keep me"* in sickness by withholding healing. No, Satan is the god of this world. He is the thief and the one responsible for the presence of sickness. Often people want to blame God for the bad things happening in this world. Instead, as the old saying goes, we should give credit where credit is due. Satan is the god of the fallen world. Blame him!

TAKING WHAT HAS ALREADY
BEEN GIVEN

The gospel of Matthew contains an interesting scripture that relates to our asserting confidence in taking/ receiving what the Lord has provided for us. It reads:

> *"And from the days of John the Baptist until now the kingdom of heaven suffereth violence, and the violent take it by force."*
>
> MATTHEW 11:12

Most commentaries, and even most translations, interpret this passage as referring to negative aggression AGAINST the kingdom. We certainly know the kingdom of heaven suffered violence during the time of John the Baptist's ministry and throughout the ministry of Jesus. One can even say that similar aggressiveness against God's kingdom continues today. However, just as violent OPPOSITION to the kingdom has always been present, so has violent PURSUIT. To exercise *"violence"* does not necessarily mean to cause injury; it can also mean to do something with passion or intensity. What then is the *"violent pursuit"* of the kingdom? It is tenacious faith – a faith that will not quit, will never give up, and will do whatever is necessary to receive what the Lord has provided.

For example, take the woman with the issue of blood. She was in *"violent pursuit"* of her healing when she pressed through the crowds to touch the garment of Jesus. Blind Bartimaeus is another. He cried out to Jesus to be healed, only to have those around him attempt to silence him. Yet, the more they tried to quiet him, the louder he cried out: *"Jesus, thou son of David, have mercy on me!"* His violent outcry of faith attracted the attention of Jesus. Take notice that for both the woman with the issue of blood and blind Bartimaeus, their violent pursuit of the kingdom OBTAINED RESULTS! Worth noting here, too, is that the Lord was not trying to withhold anything from anyone in these cases. The same is true, as well, for the numerous other examples of

His healing found in scripture. Ungodly forces were at work to obstruct and hinder the people from receiving, not Jesus.

Furthermore, releasing our faith to receive from the Lord should NOT be thought of as *"putting pressure"* on Him to answer our prayers. You do not need to force someone who has already freely given you all they have to offer! Yes, by releasing my faith, I am applying pressure to the circumstances, Satan, my body, or any other issues keeping me from my healing or miracle, but I am in no way trying to force (or convince) the Lord to heal me. When I use the phrase, *"take your healing,"* I am saying, *"reach out, pursue, and receive your healing by faith."* By doing so, you are also taking a stand against any opposing forces working to keep you from receiving. As you begin developing and renewing your mind to this way of thinking and praying, you may suddenly start saying things like *"I take that"* or *"I receive that!"* I often speak aloud when I find a good promise in God's word or when I hear a good sermon or message on something I need.

Remember, faith receives what grace has already provided. Like a radio tower, God functions as the transmitter and source of our healing. If the reception is poor, the problem is not with the strength of the signal. The issue is with me, the receiver. We need to be developed and highly trained in how to receive from the Lord. Go ahead and TAKE what He has FREELY given – do not let anything stop you!

CHAPTER 9

No Fear Here!

One aspect of faith that is essential for us to understand is that faith has the potential to become short-circuited. In the natural, a short circuit occurs when the flow of necessary power is cut off. Likewise, when walking by faith, certain things can block the flow of God's supernatural power in our life. For example, I discussed earlier how unforgiveness can hinder God's power from moving freely in our lives. Similarly, fear can also act as another short-circuit to our faith. Indeed, fear is the chief enemy of faith. If allowed to coexist in a believer's heart or mind, fear and faith will always struggle against each other. This is not to say we cannot – or will not – have *fleeting* thoughts of fear during a faith fight. However, the continued presence of strong and unwavering fear can prevent a person from receiving the full manifestation of his or her healing.

A day came during my battle for healing when the Lord spoke to me regarding fear in my own life. At the time, I was convinced I did not have any fear. After all, I had not panicked when I received the initial leukemia diagnosis. Patty and I had remained confident I would receive my healing based on the precious covenant promises of God's word. So, when the Lord confronted me about fear, I began to look more closely at my heart. While I had no fear of the illness or of death, the Spirit revealed that an element of fear WAS at work in my life, particularly regarding my family's future. I questioned how they would get by if, for some reason, I did not receive my manifestation of healing. God showed me how this uncertainty about their future was actually a form of unbelief that was working to hinder – or short-circuit – my miracle. I immediately dealt with the issue and never again considered the *"What if?"* question.

FEAR HAS A PARALYZING EFFECT. YOU CANNOT MOVE FORWARD AS LONG AS FEAR IS DOMINATING YOUR LIFE.

MORE THAN JUST AN EMOTION

Many years ago, I had an experience with fear that taught me a great lesson. A couple of friends and I were hiking in the mountains of Harlan County, Kentucky, when we came upon an old fire tower on one of the ridgetops. The tower's wooden steps had rotted away, leaving only the metal brackets behind. We decided – perhaps somewhat foolishly – to use the remaining brackets as (very small) steps to climb up the structure. My friends made their way to the top very quickly, but I was moving more slowly and began falling behind. About a quarter of the way up the tower I suddenly found myself completely paralyzed with fear. I felt like I could not go up or down – I was STUCK! Quite some time passed before I could finally shake off enough of the fear to make my way back to the ground.

I will never forget that day. I felt as if fear was controlling my entire body. Indeed, if left to itself, fear always dominates and controls, which is why God's word repeatedly commands us not to be afraid! Paul, under the inspiration of the Holy Spirit, specifically cautioned Timothy about fear, writing:

> *"For God hath not given us the spirit of fear; but of power, and of love, and of a sound mind."*
> 2 TIMOTHY 1:7

Notice Paul does not refer to fear as merely an emotion or a natural force. Fear is a spirit – one that works against the spirit of faith. During my fight of faith for healing, I had to drive fear out, and I want to encourage you to do the same. Take the promises of God and speak them against any fear present in your life. You can refuse to fear! Jesus often told people: *"fear not."* Consider the account of Jairus, found in the gospel of Luke. Scripture states Jairus sought out Jesus to heal his extremely ill daughter. However, just as Jesus was leaving to heal the girl, word came to her father that she had already died. Luke records Jesus' response to this news, writing: *"But when Jesus heard it, he answered him [Jairus], saying, Fear not: believe only, and she shall be made whole"* (Luke 8:50). The message of Jesus is simple: FEAR NOT – KEEP BELIEVING!

To keep your faith alive, you must drive out fear, and the only way to do this is by allowing the voice of God's word to become more real to you than the voice of fear. Jesus was known for rebuking people for being fearful during His earthly ministry. Notice what He said to the disciples when they found themselves in the middle of a storm and began to panic:

> *"And he [Jesus] saith unto them,*
> *Why are ye fearful, O ye of*
> *little faith? Then he arose, and*
> *rebuked the winds and the sea;*
> *and there was a great calm."*
>
> MATTHEW 8:26

Faith does not panic! Yes, this is a strong statement, but it is true. If a diagnosis from the doctor or a symptom you are experiencing sends you into a state of panic, drive fear OUT and let faith take over! Fear accomplishes nothing. Faith is the victory that overcomes! During my faith battle for healing, my motto became: *"NO FEAR HERE!"* Let those same words become real to you, too.

CHAPTER 10

What Do You Do with a Bad Report?

Let me address a question many may ask: *"What do I do if (or when) a bad report comes?"* For me, the *"bad report"* was leukemia. For you, the bad report might be cancer, heart disease, kidney failure, etc. The list goes on and on. Your response to this report can mean the difference in life or death. When faced with a battle for your physical health, you need a battle plan. What are you going to do? How are you going to respond to a negative doctor's report? In this chapter, I want to share an outline of the battle plan I used for healing. Yours may be different. Allow the Holy Spirit to direct you. He knows how best to fight and win EVERY battle.

PASTOR DALE'S BATTLE PLAN

1. Do not panic – panic is fear manifested.

2. Remind yourself DAILY of your covenant of healing.

3. Launch a counterattack on the enemy:

   - Adjust your schedule to allow extra time for God's word.
   - Consider all medical treatment plans.
   - Pray for the Holy Spirit to guide you.

4. Immerse yourself totally in the word of God:

   - Proverbs 4:20-22 says: *"My son, attend to my words; incline thine ear unto my sayings. Let them not depart from thine eyes; keep them in the midst of thine heart. For they are life unto those that find them, and health to all their flesh.*"

- Therefore, confess daily: *"God's word is healing to all my flesh. Therefore, I will spend a great amount of time reading, watching, listening to, and meditating on His word."*

5. Write down specific scriptures to form your foundation of faith.

6. Surround yourself with people of like faith:

- Use wisdom when choosing prayer partners. Choose those who will pray in faith.
- Limit the number of people you speak to about your illness, especially in the beginning.

7. Close the door on unbelief:

- You may be unable to spend time around certain people.
- You may need to avoid some family gatherings.
- Avoid participating in major conversations focusing on sickness, disease, or death.
- LIMIT the time you spend researching the illness.
- INCREASE the time you spend searching the scriptures on healing and faith.

8. Speak words of faith:

- Refuse to speak words of doubt and fear.
- Speak the promises of God aloud daily.
- Be obedient to the direction of the Holy Spirit regarding the words you should (or should not) speak.

9. Pray over all medical treatments and medications.

10. Put corresponding action with your faith:

- Remember: faith without works is dead.

People often ask me for guidance when they receive a diagnosis of serious illness. My recommendation is to consider the plan outlined in the previous pages. If I could give one piece of advice to you, it would simply be to spend an EXCESSIVE amount of time in God's word! You cannot spend too much time in scripture. God's medicine has no harmful side effects. Indeed, the only side-effects you can expect from taking a *"high dosage"* of His word are good ones. You could even be spending time meditating on healing and suddenly find yourself being blessed in some other area of your life!

I also encourage you to keep up the good fight of faith even after you receive your manifestation of healing. I recommend you MAINTAIN healing by faith by continuing to allow God's word to be medicine to you.

To this day, I still make healing confessions. I consistently watch specific healing programs weekly to feed my faith for healing. Now that I am healed, I do not plan to allow the enemy any opportunity to return. I encourage you to do the same! Close the door on sickness – and keep it closed!

CHAPTER 11

Satan's Counterattack

One thing is for sure: Satan always looks for an opportunity to make a comeback. Jesus warned of this when He spoke about demons attempting to return to the person from whom they had been expelled:

> *"When an unclean spirit goes out of a man, he goes through dry places, seeking rest; and finding none, he says, 'I will return to my house from*

which I came.' And when he comes, he finds it swept and put in order. Then he goes and takes with him seven other spirits more wicked than himself, and they enter and dwell there; and the last state of that man is worse than the first."

LUKE 11:24-27 (NKJV)

Notice the devil says, *"I will return to the house from which I came."* Satan is never happy about being removed or displaced from a person's life, and he despises seeing people delivered and set free from the effects of his works, including sickness. Satan desires for you to stay sick! He always opposes healing. Because of this, once we receive the manifestation of healing in our bodies, we should <u>not</u> consider it a strange occurrence if (or when) sickness tries to return.

In May 2020, I experienced this type of counterattack from the enemy. I was going along enjoying life just as my doctor had prescribed. I had experienced no symptoms of leukemia since the Lord moved for me in 2017, and all my labs were completely normal. Our in-house church services had just relaunched after being closed due to statewide Covid-19-related mandates. Our schedule at the time consisted of two Sunday morning services and a Wednesday night online session. I felt fine, albeit I was extremely busy with our relaunch. One morning while looking in the mirror, I noticed my facial coloring did not seem quite right. I had also recently begun to experience a few other minor issues, but none seemed too concerning.

The next day, I asked Patty if she had noticed anything different about my skin tone. She had not, but she told me our daughter, Mikaela, had mentioned my coloration to her. I still did not think much of the change. However, after a few more days, I began to encounter another level of symptoms. This time I could not deny I was experiencing issues similar to those I had previously encountered when my blood levels dropped from leukemia. I decided to make a call and set up an appointment with my oncologist, the wonderful doctor to whom God had directed me earlier and through whom He had worked mightily to heal me. I knew the protocol: have my blood drawn, send that blood to the doctor's office in Lexington, then wait for his call. We had repeated this procedure many times before, and I knew from previous experience that an immediate call back from his office meant we needed to act quickly. In contrast, a delayed call meant they had found no significant issues.

My cellphone rang within just a few hours of having the blood drawn, and the message was clear and much too familiar: *"Your hemoglobin has dropped, and you need blood immediately."* I had gone to Lexington for blood transfusions in the past, but now Covid-19 restrictions had many facilities shut down. So, I opted to use the local outpatient services and had the blood I needed within twenty-four hours. I received the transfusion on Thursday, and my doctor planned to see me in Lexington the following Tuesday. Despite the unexpectedness of the circumstances, I had complete peace about everything.

I stayed busy on Saturday preparing for our two upcoming Sunday morning services. Not surprisingly, my greatest battles seem to come on the weekend, as I am sure Satan hates Sundays with a passion. Although I was again experiencing some weakness and other symptoms, I was not about to be defeated. I had an intense headache and was so weak that getting dressed took extra time. While most people in my condition would not have attempted to attend, I had already resolved in my mind not to miss church! I spoke with Patty about sharing a testimony during a portion of my sermon time, and once I arrived at the church, I stayed in my office until worship began. Then I joined the congregation and worshipped as always. Even though doing so was not easy, I stood and praised the Lord with everything in me, as this was my way of letting the devil know I did not intend to be defeated. When my time to speak came, I entered the pulpit for both services. I did my part and then called for Patty to come share a word and close the service. Despite the difficulties, we pushed through with the aid of God's strength working in me.

The fact I was in a significant battle became even more apparent as the day progressed, and by Sunday afternoon, I found myself confronted with a major decision. I knew I was healed by the stripes of Jesus, and no doubt of that fact was in my mind. Despite my current circumstances, I was convinced and entirely at peace with having already been healed. However, Patty looked at me and said: *"We can fight this battle at the hospital the same as here at home."* I now had to choose: would I fight the good fight of faith at home, or would I seek medical help? In pondering this, the Lord reminded me of a great healing message from Greg Mohr in which he speaks of how our bodies do not belong to us. Instead, our bodies belong first to the

Lord if we are saved and second to our spouses if we are married. Based upon what I learned from brother Mohr, I submitted to my wife's request to go and have labs conducted at the local emergency room.

When we arrived at the ER, I quickly explained my situation to the attending physician. I expected they would want to do many tests, but I already knew what was happening in my body. I had been in this situation before. They performed a CBC, and the results confirmed my suspicions: the blood I received earlier in the week had not kept my hemoglobin at a safe level. My hemoglobin was now in the mid to upper 4s, with an average range being 13-16. Most people cannot even function at a level as low as 4 or 5. So when I told them I had been to church and stood to minister twice that morning, they were stunned! After contacting and consulting with my doctor, they swiftly decided to admit me to St. Joseph Hospital in Lexington for an emergency blood transfusion.

We opted to go to Lexington instead of staying in London because of an issue with my blood type. Due to the number of transfusions that I received during my initial battle with leukemia, I developed antibodies in my blood that made finding a match for me very difficult. We believed the process would be quicker in Lexington, and I did not have time to wait due to my extremely low hemoglobin levels. When I told the ER doctor my wife would drive me to Lexington, he looked at me in disbelief and said: *"No. You need to go by ambulance, and it will need to be equipped with advanced life support."* The medical professionals were obviously more concerned about my condition than I was.

Within the hour, I was on my way to the hospital in Lexington. While being loaded into the ambulance, I remember sensing the abundance of God's peace upon me. I laid back and rested for the one-hour trip. A few weeks before this battle, I experienced something from the Lord I consider of utmost importance and worthy of noting. While lying in bed one night, God's great peace came over me, and He began to speak to me about resting in Him and finding rest in His word.

IN THAT MOMENT, GOD GAVE ME A GREATER REVELATION OF THE **UNPARALLELED REST** THAT FAITH IN HIS PROMISES BRINGS. THE PEACE OFFERED BY THE WORLD IS SIMPLY **NO** COMPARISON.

Looking back on that night, I believe God was providing me with a specific strategy for the coming fight. Indeed, one must always be mindful that God's plan often differs from one battle to the next. For example, this was not the first time I had been rushed to Lexington for an emergency blood transfusion. During my first experience, Patty and I were actively engaged in warfare the entire time. We spoke the word and prayed in the Spirit almost all night long, which was God's strategy for THAT specific fight. However, God's directive for this present battle was not one of staying up all night praying or speaking the word. Instead, His strategy was for me to simply *"rest"* in faith, which is precisely what I did. As I made the ambulance trip to Lexington, I laid back and rested according to the word spoken to me by the Lord just a few weeks prior.

Like those in London, the hospital personnel in Lexington seemed extremely alarmed by my condition when I arrived. The nurse in charge was especially troubled by the difficulty in finding a blood type compatible with mine. After several hours of waiting for a match, I followed the Lord's directions to *"rest"* and went to sleep. Much like David slept and rested even when his enemies were seeking to take his life, I was able to partake in the great rest that comes from assurance in God and His word!

As the issues locating compatible blood continued, the lead nurse became even more alarmed. During the middle of the night, she came in to share her concerns. Unlike the nurse, I was at complete ease regarding my condition – to the point that she had to wake me up to update me on the situation. As the nurse entered my room, Patty said something aloud in prayer. Thinking Patty had spoken to her, the nurse asked her what she had said, to which Patty replied: *"Oh, I was just praying."* After sharing her concerns, the nurse left the room but returned just a short time later and excitedly declared: *"Your prayers have worked! Your blood is on the way."* By morning I had received the blood transfusion, and by the afternoon, I was back home in London doing well.

I am fully convinced this episode was a counterattack of the enemy – an attempt to return and finish the devastation he tried to bring upon my body a few years earlier. A great scripture is found in Nahum to use against sickness when it attempts to make a comeback:

> *"What do you conspire against the Lord? He will make an utter end of it. Affliction will not rise up a second time."*
>
> NAHUM 1:9 (NKJV)

In other translations, the second half of this verse reads:

- *"Suffering shall not arise a second time."*
- *"Affliction shall not rise up a second time."*
- *"Oppression shall not rise up a second time."*
- *"There shall not rise a double affliction."*
- *"Adversity will not strike twice."*
- *"No opponent rises a second time."*
- *"Distress will not rise up twice."*

According to God's word, sickness and disease ARE forms of oppression! The writer of Acts speaks of how *"God anointed Jesus of Nazareth with the Holy Spirit and with power, who went about doing good* *and healing all who were **OPPRESSED** <u>by the devil,</u> for God was with Him."* (Acts 10:38 NKJV) I had already been through oppression/affliction/adversity/ distress from the devil and received my healing. This attempted comeback by leukemia was merely affliction and oppression trying to *"rise up"* a second time. However, according to Nahum 1:9, this affliction from the enemy had no right to return. Praise God!

Indeed, keeping my confession in line with the word of God was incredibly important in my overcoming Satan's attempted comeback. Even when symptoms returned and the doctors' reports were not the most encouraging, I did not change my profession of faith for healing. I never made statements like: *"well, I guess this cancer has just returned"* or *"I suppose I didn't really get healed."* No! My confession remained consistent: *"I am a covenant person and, by His stripes, I am healed."* Healing is in my covenant, and that covenant is signed, sealed, and delivered by the blood of Jesus. Therefore, I am healed! God's covenant is surer than any contract or binding agreement in this world. Regardless of what my body or any doctor's report said, I had the word of my covenant to stand upon – and THAT is the report I chose to believe.

In addition to aligning my confession with the word, I continued to be sensitive to the Lord's leading, even with my medical treatment. As I shared earlier, God initially directed me to my current oncologist in 2017. When he and I first met, I heard the Lord say in my spirit: *"Follow his directions. Do what he tells you to do."* This doctor and I have always been able to come into agreement regarding my care. If I did not feel led to participate in a specific treatment, he would honor my feelings with no pressure to comply. After being released from the hospital on Monday, I had an appointment to see my oncologist the following day, which would be my first time seeing him since the reoccurrence. Having received no new instructions from the Lord, I still felt led to follow the doctor's orders, despite not knowing what he might recommend.

On Tuesday morning, I visited the oncology diagnostic imaging facility for the first time since receiving my healing from the Lord in 2017. The experience felt almost like history repeating itself as they placed me in the tightly enclosed machine and began the scans that would allow the professionals to see what was happening inside my body. After lunch, my doctor and I were to meet and go over the results. Through all of this, I continued to rest in the Lord!

I arrived for my oncology appointment at 1 PM, eager to meet with the man God had used many times before to aid in healing my body. The reports indicated the leukemia was attempting to rise up again. However, the scans found no issues with my organs, nor did they show any of the numerous indicators that were evident during my initial diagnosis in 2015. Instead, I was experiencing anemia, a condition sometimes associated with CLL. My doctor did not seem nearly as concerned as the other medical professionals I had encountered in recent days. He simply stated: *"God has given us a wonderful medication that should take care of this condition and keep this anemia from happening again.*" However, the last thing I wanted to do was take medication. Up until this point, the Lord had sustained my health without it. Now I was confronted with a choice in my faith walk: deny medication and fight with faith alone or take the medication in combination WITH my faith. Something I have learned over the years is that all healing – and any aid TO healing – comes from the Lord. Doctors cannot heal. They can only assist your body in being healed. The Lord is the source of all true healing.

When my doctor said God had provided a great medication to treat the issue, I could not deny the wisdom God gave scientists to create such a medicine. Bearing in mind, too, God's instructions to me to *"follow the directions this doctor gives,"* I decided to comply with my oncologist's recommendation and began the medication within the week. When I started the new medicine, I followed a specific routine by praying daily over the pill and declaring: *"I receive the wisdom God has placed within this medication. It will bless my body and not harm it, and I refuse all negative side effects."* Two years later, I still make the same confession daily. Three months after beginning the new regime, I saw my doctor again. He quickly confirmed the medicine was working as designed. However, God delights in doing MORE THAN the expected. Although a *"low normal"* hemoglobin level is around 13.5, my doctor only anticipated my levels would rise to about 12. Yet today, my hemoglobin averages around 16. With God working through faith, the medication does much more than expected. Furthermore, I have no signs of active anemia or other conditions associated with leukemia working in my body. Praise God!

Always remember to stand firm in your faith when the enemy attempts a counterattack. Do not cast away your confidence. Hold fast to God's promises and keep faith alive and active. You can overcome – and win!

CHAPTER 12

Sustained in Sickness and Disease

As I was preparing to finish this book, the Lord spoke to me about adding one more chapter to help bring further clarity on receiving healing by faith. We must always be mindful that this is a *"faith fight"* and that biblical faith is not shaken or moved by what we see or feel. No, biblical faith is built securely upon the unchanging foundation of God's Word. His promises are true REGARDLESS of our present circumstances! However, because this is a journey of faith, we are not given an estimated time or date of arrival. Some manifestations of faith come quickly, while others are delayed. Our faith must remain steady through every season, despite whether we see results manifesting or if nothing seems to be occurring right now. I have experienced this in my own healing faith journey and as I draw this book to a close, allow me to share some things that have significantly helped me move forward with healing.

GOD'S SUSTAINING POWER

As we have already established, divine healing does not always come to us in its fully completed form – at least not initially. Sometimes we receive our healing in stages, and during the seasons of waiting we often experience what I refer to as God's *"sustaining power"* for healing. In 1 Kings, the Lord tells Elijah:

> *"Arise, get thee to Zarephath,*
> *which belongeth to Zidon, and*
> *dwell there: behold, I have*

commanded a widow woman

there to <u>sustain</u> thee."

In this context, *"sustain"* means to maintain, contain, support, or nourish. Here the term also means *"to be supplied."* God tells Elijah that He has called upon the widow to provide Elijah with enough nourishment and strength to support and maintain him on the journey. Because of God's *"sustaining power,"* Elijah had what he needed to see his journey through.

Over the years, I have discovered that the Lord often provides His *"sustaining power"* as part of our healing journey. Even if you do not yet have the full manifestation of your healing, do not be defeated or overcome. God's sustaining power will provide you with the strength and health necessary to continue living the life He intended you to live. The book of Nehemiah also mentions the sustaining power of God. When speaking of God caring for the children of Israel, Nehemiah writes:

"Forty years You sustained

them in the wilderness;

They lacked nothing; Their

clothes did not wear out And

their feet did not swell."

NEHEMIAH 9:21 (NKJV)

The Israelites experienced God's sustaining power while traveling forty years in the wilderness. His power kept them from lack, even sustaining their clothes by keeping them in usable condition for forty years! Simply amazing, right? Not only that, but the Lord also kept their feet healthy and strong enough to walk many miles through the desert.

God is able and willing to do the same for us regarding our bodies. If the full manifestation of your healing does not occur immediately, use your faith to believe for God's sustaining power. This power will allow you to keep getting out of bed every morning and give you the strength to keep doing what you need to do in everyday life. God's sustaining power will keep you alive! For example, many years ago, we were told my father-in-law had only about six months to live due to an extreme heart issue. He needed a heart transplant but could not receive one because of other major health problems. Yet, amazingly, despite his doctors' grim prognosis, he lived many more years with the condition. God's grace, coupled with His sustaining power, kept my father-in-law alive.

In the Bible, David often speaks of being sustained by God's power. In Psalm 3, he says:

> "Lord, how are they increased that trouble me! many are they that rise up against me. Many there be which say of my soul, There is no help for him in God. Selah. But thou, O Lord, art a shield for me; my glory, and the lifter up of mine head. I cried unto the Lord with my voice,

and he heard me out of his holy hill.

Selah. I laid me down and slept; I

awaked; <u>for the Lord sustained me</u>."

PSALM 3:1-5

Despite being chased by numerous enemies, the Lord sustained and kept him – even as he slept. Like the men who pursued David, sickness is an enemy. Just as David's foes sought to take him out, sickness attempts to steal our health, often to the point of taking our lives. In my battle with leukemia, sickness tried to take me out. Yet, like David, God's sustaining power kept me alive. In another passage, David declares: *"Cast thy burden upon the Lord and He shall sustain thee"* (Psalm 55:22). David knew the Lord had sustained his life repeatedly. Pause and reflect on how many times the Lord has sustained YOU over the years. He is willing to do it again! When I experienced disease and sickness that should have taken me out, I survived. Why? God's sustaining power. How many testimonies have you heard where someone who should have died instead lived? How often have doctors given up hope but, suddenly, the person fully recovers? God gives us <u>sustaining</u> power.

THE LITTLE STEPS

Perhaps you are believing for complete healing. Continue to believe. Wholeness is undoubtedly God's will for our lives. Keep tapping into His sustaining power until you experience the full manifestation of your healing. Like David, keep praising God every day when you awaken. Keep thanking Him for the healing strength working in your body little by little. Celebrate every small step forward. Ultimately, those *"little steps"* of healing fueled by God's sustaining power and planted firmly on His word are what will lead you to victory in YOUR healing faith journey!

CHAPTER 13

Healing Scriptures and Confessions

The following verses are from the list of healing scriptures I personally used when standing by faith for my healing of leukemia. I have also included confessions to make in conjunction with these Bible promises if you so desire. Speak these scriptures aloud often and with EXPECTATION that the living word of God will produce a harvest of healing in your life.

"...if thou wilt diligently hearken to the voice of the LORD thy God, and wilt do that which is right in his sight, and wilt give ear to his commandments, and keep all his statutes, I will put none of these diseases upon thee, which I have brought upon the Egyptians: for I am the LORD that healeth thee."

EXODUS 15:26

"And the Lord will take away from thee all sickness, and will put none of the evil diseases of Egypt, which thou knowest, upon thee; but will lay them upon all them that hate thee."

DEUTERONOMY 7:15

CONFESSION 1: Father, I thank You that none of the diseases of Egypt will come upon me; for you are the Lord who heals me!

*"And ye shall serve the LORD
your God, and he shall bless
thy bread, and thy water;
and I will take sickness away
from the midst of thee."*

EXODUS 23:25

CONFESSION 2: God has blessed my food and water. He has taken ALL sickness from my presence.

*"I call heaven and earth to
record this day against you,
that I have set before you life
and death, blessing and cursing:
therefore choose life, that both
thou and thy seed may live..."*

DEUTERONOMY 30:19

CONFESSION 3: I reject death and choose life. I reject every form of the curse and choose the blessing so my children and I may live!

"Concerning the works of men, By the word of Your lips, I have kept away from the paths of the destroyer."

PSALM 17:4 (NKJV)

CONFESSION 4: The power of Your word keeps me from the destroyer. Sickness is a destroyer, and Your word will keep me from its destruction.

"God is our refuge and strength, a very present help in trouble."

PSALM 46:1

CONFESSION 5: God is my refuge and strength during this battle with sickness. He is present with me to help me completely overcome this illness.

"Bless the Lord, O my soul; And all that is within me, bless His holy name! Bless the Lord, O my soul, And forget not all His benefits: Who forgives all your iniquities, Who heals all your diseases, Who redeems your life from destruction, Who crowns you with lovingkindness and tender mercies, Who satisfies your mouth with good things, So that your youth is renewed like the eagle's."

PSALM 103:1-5 (NKJV)

CONFESSION 6: I will remember and never forget all my benefits. God has forgiven me of all sin. He has healed all my diseases. God has redeemed my life from all destruction and crowned me with His lovingkindness and mercies. God has satisfied my mouth with good things. He has renewed my youth like the eagle's.

"My son, attend to my words; incline thine ear unto my sayings. Let them not depart from thine eyes; keep them in the midst of thine heart. For they are life unto those that find them, and health to all their flesh."

PROVERBS 4:20-22

CONFESSION 7: I give my attention to Your word. I incline my ear (lean in and listen) to Your sayings. I do not allow Your word to depart from my eyes. I always keep Your word in my heart. Your words are life and health to all my flesh as I meditate on them.

"A man's spirit will sustain him in sickness, but a crushed spirit, who can bear?"

PROVERBS 18:14 (WEB)

CONFESSION 8: My spirit is strong in the Lord and will sustain and keep me in the time of sickness! I am strong in the Lord!

"Surely he hath borne our <u>griefs</u>, and carried our <u>sorrows</u>: yet we did esteem him stricken, smitten of God, and afflicted. But he was wounded for our transgressions, he was bruised for our iniquities: the chastisement of our peace was upon him; and with his stripes we are healed."

ISAIAH 53:4-5

* Note in the original language that "griefs" and "sorrows" may be translated as "sickness" and "pain."

"...who Himself bore our sins in His own body on the tree, that we, having died to sins, might live for righteousness — by whose stripes you were healed."

1 PETER 2:24

CONFESSION 9: Jesus has borne (taken) all my sickness and carried all my pain. Therefore, I do not allow sickness or pain to dwell in my body. By His stripes, I am healed!

"When evening had come, they brought to Him many who were demon-possessed. And He cast out the spirits with a word, and healed all who were sick, that it might be fulfilled which was spoken by Isaiah the prophet, saying: 'He Himself took our infirmities And bore our sicknesses'."

MATTHEW 8:16 (NKJV)

CONFESSION 10: Jesus healed ALL who were sick. Therefore, healing is His will for me.

"And Jesus went forth, and saw a great multitude, and was moved with compassion toward them, and he healed their sick."

MATTHEW 14:14

CONFESSION 11: Jesus is compassionate toward me during this time of sickness. I receive His compassion and take His healing!

"Beloved, I wish above all things that thou mayest prosper and be in health, even as thy soul prospereth."

3 JOHN 2

CONFESSION 12: God's will for me is to prosper and be healthy in both my body and soul. Sickness is not God's plan for me.

"How God anointed Jesus of Nazareth with the Holy Ghost and with power: who went about doing good, and healing all that were oppressed of the devil; for God was with him."

ACTS 10:38

CONFESSION 13: The works of Jesus included doing good and healing ALL who were oppressed of the devil. Sickness is oppression and is of the devil. Therefore, Jesus makes me free from all sickness and disease!

"For this purpose the Son of God was manifested, that he might destroy the works of the devil."

1 JOHN 3:8b

CONFESSION 14: Jesus came to destroy all works of the devil, including sickness. This sickness is powerless against what Jesus has already provided for me.

"He sent his word, and healed them, and delivered them from their destruction."

PSALM 107:20

CONFESSION 15: God sent His word to heal me. As I meditate upon His promises, His word brings healing to every part of my body. Sickness is destruction, and God's word is delivering me from ALL destruction.

"With long life will I satisfy him,
and shew him my salvation."

PSALM 91:16

CONFESSION 16: Thank you, Lord, I will not die prematurely, but You will satisfy me with long life.

"I shall not die, but live, and
declare the works of the Lord."

PSALM 118:17

CONFESSION 17: I will not die from this sickness. I will live, and my healing will be a testimony of the works of the Lord.

"Let us hold fast the profession of
our faith without wavering; (for
he is faithful that promised)."

HEBREWS 10:23

CONFESSION 18: I am unshakeable in my healing confession, and I will not waver. Jesus promised healing, and He is faithful to keep His promises.

"For all the promises of God in him are yea, and in him Amen, unto the glory of God by us."

2 CORINTHIANS 1:20

CONFESSION 19: Lord, I take You at Your word and receive Your promises for me regarding healing. You have said *"yes"* to healing, and I say *"amen"* (so be it).

"No weapon that is formed against thee shall prosper; and every tongue that shall rise against thee in judgment thou shalt condemn. This is the heritage of the servants of the Lord, and their righteousness is of me, saith the Lord."

ISAIAH 54:17

CONFESSION 20: No weapon of sickness will prosper in my body. No words of sickness that rise against me shall prevail. Because I am a servant of the Lord, healing is my heritage.

"Now this is the confidence that we have in Him, that if we ask anything according to His will, He hears us. And if we know that He hears us, whatever we ask, we know that we have the petitions that we have asked of Him."

1 JOHN 5:14-15 (NKJV)

CONFESSION 21: I am confident I am praying the will of God when I pray His word. When I pray His will, He hears and answers my request.

"For the LORD God is a sun and shield: the LORD will give grace and glory: no good thing will he withhold from them that walk uprightly."

PSALM 84:11 (NKJV)

CONFESSION 22: Healing is a good thing, and God will not withhold anything good from me.

"Jesus Christ the same yesterday,
and today, and forever."

HEBREWS 13:8

CONFESSION 23: Jesus healed and provided deliverance while He was on the earth, and He is still doing so today. Jesus, I receive Your healing.

"Fear not, for I am with you; Be
not dismayed, for I am your God.
I will strengthen you, Yes, I will
help you, I will uphold you with
My righteous right hand."

ISAIAH 41:10 (NKJV)

CONFESSION 24: I will not fear. I know God is with me. He is strengthening, helping, and upholding me during this time.

"For I am the Lord, I change not..."

MALACHI 3:6

CONFESSION 25: God has always provided healing for His people in the Old and New Covenants. He has not changed, and healing is for me.

"The thief does not come except to steal, and to kill, and to destroy. I have come that they may have life, and that they may have it more abundantly."

JOHN 10:10 (NKJV)

CONFESSION 26: Sickness is a thief, and I do not allow it to steal, kill, or bring destruction to me. I receive the abundant life Jesus made available to me.

"Submit yourselves therefore to God. Resist the devil, and he will flee from you."

CONFESSION 27: I submit myself to God and His word. I resist (stand firm against) the devil and all sickness, and he must flee.

"For God hath not given us the spirit of fear; but of power, and of love, and of a sound mind."

2 TIMOTHY 1:7

CONFESSION 28: Fear is not from God. I will not allow fear to have any place in my life. Fear and sickness both must go!

ADDENDUM

Additional Resources

We pray this book has been a blessing to you on your journey toward health and wholeness. For additional information on biblical healing, Grace Fellowship Church offers several free resources, including an online Healing Library featuring links to past years' sessions of the annual GFC Healing School, taught by Pastor Dale, as well as other tools. In addition, the church's archive of weekly messages is freely accessible on various digital platforms, including the Grace Fellowship website, the

GraceCast podcast feeds, and the free GFC mobile app for iOS and Android devices. Use the following links to find out more:

- *Healing Library:*

  GRACEFOR**YOU**.COM/**HEALING**

- *GFC Website:*

  GRACEFOR**YOU**.COM

- *Download the App:*

  GRACEFOR**YOU**.COM/**GET-THE-APP**

Follow Grace Fellowship on social media or subscribe to the GFC podcasts, YouTube, or Roku channels, by searching: Grace Fellowship - London. To contact Pastor Dale directly:

PASTORDALE@**GRACE**FOR**YOU**.COM

Grace Fellowship Church
911 TLC Lane
London, KY 40741

P: 606-864-4635

SCAN TO DOWNLOAD THE GFC APP: